# Heart Like a Starfish

## Allen Callaci

*Heart Like A Starfish* by Allen Callaci

ISBN-10: 1938349350
ISBN-13: 978-1-938349-35-5
eISBN: 978-1-938349-38-6
Library of Congress Control Number: 2015955275

Copyright © 2016 Allen Callaci

This work is licensed under the Creative Commons Attribution-NonCommercial-NoDerivatives 4.0 International License. To view a copy of this license, visit http://creativecommons.org/licenses/by-nc-nd/4.0/.

Cover illustration, interior ornamentations and illustrations by Amy Maloof
All other illustrations by Allen Callaci
Author photo by Marc Campos
Layout and Book Design by Mark Givens

First Pelekinesis Printing 2016

For information:
Pelekinesis, 112 Harvard Ave #65, Claremont, CA 91711 USA

www.pelekinesis.com

# Heart like a Starfish

ALLEN CALLACI

Excerpt(s) from LET'S TAKE THE LONG WAY HOME: A MEMOIR OF FRIENDSHIP by Gail Caldwell, copyright © 2010 by Gail Caldwell. Used by permission of Random House, an imprint and division of Penguin Random House LLC. All rights reserved.

Excerpt(s) from LONESOME SURPRISE and ONE OF EVERYTHING by Refrigerator. Written by Allen Callaci. Used by permission of the artist and Shrimper. All rights reserved.

Excerpt(s) from BE POSITIVE and TURN TO THE STARS WHEN YOU'RE GREY by Refrigerator. Written by Dennis Callaci. Used by permission of the artist and Shrimper. All rights reserved.

Excerpt(s) from VULNERABLE SLEEP. Written by Adam Lipman. Used by permission of the artist and Shrimper. All rights reserved.

Excerpt from NIGHT LIGHT by The Mountain Goats. Written by John Darnielle. copyright © 2012 Cadmean Dawn, administered by Pacific Electric. Used by permission. All rights reserved.

Excerpt from THIS YEAR by The Mountain Goats. Written by John Darnielle. copyright © 2004 Cadmean Dawn, administered by Pacific Electric. Used by permission. All rights reserved.

# PRAISE FOR ALLEN CALLACI

"A true hero's journey, Callaci's memoir is layered with symbols along the path to help guide the narrator and reader. A dry, Han Solo-like humor helps us get through the heartbreak. And like a Shakespearean dream, we awaken at the end with newfound joy, cherishing this wonderful life."

—Kevin Glavin, author of *Rock Star's Rainbow* and *All The Things You'll Do!*

"Allen shares his amazing story by locating his personal experience in the midst of a network of relationships that sustain and define his life. He spins a web of love that shows an ability to connect with others that makes it abundantly clear how he was able to muster the strength to make it through his ordeal. He also spins a web in time that moves effortlessly back and forth across the full spectrum of his life experience in a circular rhythm that never makes you feel like you're lost. Instead, you feel like you're being taken for a spin by a great friend across the Southern California landscape he narrates so deftly. The title seems to call our attention to the remarkable contrast between the failure of the physical heart Allen was born with and the success of the spiritual heart that comes through on every page here. Thank you Allen!"

—John Davis, recording artist (Shrimper Records, Folk Implosion, johnhdavis.com)

"For any generation... An astonishing story about how close life is to death. Written in a relatable style...Existential...using street language...Callaci's true story is heartfelt!!"

—Claudia Lennear, featured backup singer in the Academy Award winning documentary *20 Feet From Stardom*

*For Dennis, Loretta, and Jen - this is as much your story as it is mine.*

*… and a special shout out to Prednisone for keeping me strung out until 5 am all those nights so I could get this all down …*

*"Like a starfish, the heart endures its amputation."*
*Gail Caldwell*

# DARK SHADOWS

## STARTS, STOPS, AND STARTS.

Conscious again. Looking at yourself, your reflection. How many pounds have you lost? 20…25…30? Your goatee has gone all ZZ Top. Your arms are pencil thin. Dozens of IV lines protrude out from your body like tentacles. Your stomach and chest is a tightly bandaged dead field of staples, stitches and dried brown bloody blotches.

*Where am I?*

Your fingernails and toenails have grown into claws. You look down at your feet. They look like they could be Yoda's.

*WHERE THE FUCK AM I?*

*How long have I been out?*

*Weeks?*

*Months?*

*Years?*

*Is Obama still president?*

*whereamI?…where am I?…WHERE-AM-I?..*

You get no response to the questions frenetically ping-ponging from one side of your mind to the other, only the discomfiting muffled, distorted beep coming from the medical monitor to your left.

WHAT'S WRONG WITH ME?... WHAT'S WRONG WITH ME?... WHAT'S WRONG WITH ME?

*...where am I...*

*...where am I...*

*...where am I...*

The medical monitor lets out another muffled cry.

Confused, salty tears begin to form in the ducts of your swollen eyes.

*How did I end up here?*

I awaken on the bathroom floor with a slightly bleeding tongue. I must have bit down on it when I blacked out. I must have blacked out hard. I grab the side of the white porcelain toilet bowl to hoist myself up. Still dizzy I look down at the cold white tiles. There is no blood.

No, no blood.

*Thank God.*

I've never been one for doctors except for Dr. Seuss, Dr. Who and Dr. Bones McCoy from the original *Star Trek* series, but as I gaze at my colorless reflection in the tiny medicine cabinet mirror I know I'm in need of some serious medical attention.

Don't panic.

**MAINTAIN.**

**MAINTAIN.**

maintain

*Holy shit what would have happened had I passed out like this while driving home on the freeway?...what's happening I've never even really* been sick…*thank God my head didn't crack itself wide open like an egg when I hit the tile…please God don't let this be anything serious…*I take out my cell and leave messages with my younger brother, Dennis, and older sister, Loretta, letting them know I'm not feeling well and looking for a lift to go to Urgent Care…*please God don't let this be anything serious…*

And then I call **her**. Things have never been as strained between us as they've been lately but I call and she picks up. I tell her as much as I can as gently as I can: I went to work… I left early… not feeling right but hoping it's nothing…would she mind driving me to Urgent Care? I should say more. I should at least tell her the part about blacking out across the bathroom tiles. I know. But I also know Jen. I know how much she worries and how fiercely she internalizes those worries. " I'll be right over," she says in a frightened hush, "… stay right where you are."

*…please God don't let this be anything serious…*

Jen arrives. She looks at me and looks every bit as worried as I was afraid she would be. I could say something to her but I don't. Neither of us want to go there.

"Where's your medical card?"

"I don't know."

"What do you mean you don't know?" Her eyes roll. "They're not going to see you at Urgent Care without your medical card."

"It'll work out. It always does."

"You're really unbelievable," she says with an exasperated sigh. "Were you even able to eat something and keep it down today?"

I tell her about the strawberry smoothie and the slice of pizza I just couldn't finish.

"And how nutritious does all this sound to you?"

"A strawberry smoothie doesn't sound completely unhealthy to me."

"It doesn't? Unless you made that smoothie yourself–which I know you didn't–it's probably got 30 plus grams of sugar in it."

God, how she worries.

"But smoothies seem healthy. Strawberries are healthy. Whoever thought there'd be tons of sugar in a Starbucks strawberry smoothie?"

"What am I going to do with you?" she responds tugging at the windshield visor as her eyes once again roll reflexively to the back of her head. I can't help but laugh at her patented eye roll as if I were watching a favorite episode of *Seinfeld*.

She lets my laughter float a solid 3 seconds.

"Are **YOU** done?"

"I'm just trying to bring a little levity, Jen."

"Stop."

6 months later I will receive a not-so-subtle e-mail from her:

> I looked it up online. There are exactly 41 GRAMS!!! of sugar in a Starbucks strawberry smoothie. Just thought you should know.
> -Jen.

Some people say we act like an old married couple.

We're not.

We're as different as The Beatles and The Stones. She is "You Can't Always Get What You Want" to my "Strawberry Fields." She is a healthcare professional at the nationally renowned City of Hope. She knows her shit. I know her frustration. I am the farthest thing from being a healthcare professional at a nationally renowned hospital. I sing in a lo-fi rock 'n' roll band that defiantly issues its music to a non-waiting world on dead formats such as cassettes and vinyl. As with so many other rock 'n' roll singers you may have heard of, I spend my downtime between recording, live shows, and supermodels working at a public library and teaching English part-time at the local community college.

I can deconstruct any passage from *Anna Karenina* you care to throw at me but when it comes to the world of medicine it's a language I've never learned. I have learned a separate language. One that sees signs, loaded meanings, and hidden metaphors everywhere and in everything: Jen's car that takes me to the Urgent Care is a perfect example of this tendency. It's an Isuzu "Ascender."

To Ascend.

To rise from a lower plane to a higher one.

Jen's Ascender is silent the rest of the way to Urgent Care save for the sound of Aretha Franklin singing "Let the Good Times Roll" from a CD mix I burned for her a lifetime ago.

Urgent Care will be closing in 20 minutes. It is a cramped rectangular building located in the corner of a poorly planned stew of a strip mall: A Chinese buffet, an Aaron Brothers, and a THERE IS HOPE foster agency.

There is nobody else in the waiting area besides Jen and myself. *Dancing With the Stars* plays on the small waiting room TV. While Bristol Palin dances on I make the necessary calls and stay on hold the necessary time tracking down my medical card number. Jen's eyes stay anxiously fixated on her phone.

"I told you they weren't going to see you without your medical card, didn't I?" she mutters under her breath. "We should have gone to the ER."

*I see how fragile and concerned she is.*

*She thinks I can't.*

*I can.*

My sister Loretta and Harmonie, my 14 year-old niece, join us at Urgent Care. Harmonie is excited. She actually gets to watch *Dancing With the Stars* tonight. "Oh my God," she exclaims flicking her sandy blonde hair. "My mom never lets me watch this show!" Harmonie's *Dancing With The Stars* excitement is tempered by Loretta's concern. She hugs me tighter and longer than usual and wants to know exactly what's going on. I tell her what little there is I know. I wish there were more.

I wonder what my brother Dennis is going to make of all this. If our roles were reversed I'd want to know something/anything and know it now. I'd want all the guaranteed reassurance I could get that everything would be snapping right back to the way it was by sunrise. I'd want to hear that come Sunday we'll all be gathered round Loretta's table, like last Sunday and the hundred Sundays before that, surrounded by orange juice, strawberries, French toast and each other.

I so can't wait to be the hell out of here.

I can't.

My God, what a pain in the ass it all is. The magazines. The cramped padded chairs. The forms. Now I know why I've always been so averse to doctor visits. This is limbo. I wish I could just type "why the hell did I pass out across my bathroom floor earlier today" into Google and get an instantaneous answer.

*Don't think about it too much. Don't say too much out loud. You don't want to scare Harmonie.*

*You don't want to scare yourself.*

They take me back. Draw some blood. Ask their questions: "Does this hurt? What about this? What about now?" They think it's the appendix. I'm no medical expert by any means—I'm certainly not Jen—but I know it's not my appendix. Still they keep pressing down and asking how it feels and I keep answering "like nothing really." They don't believe me. They are closing for the evening and want me sent to San Antonio Hospital overnight in case the appendix bursts. Jen is in the process of moving and going back east in a few days to check in on her sister who just had thyroid surgery. She's got a world going on as always. The plan becomes for Jen to go home and drop Harmonie off at Dennis' while Loretta and I make our way east to San Antonio Hospital.

"Buckle up, little brother," Loretta calls to me in a light nervous tone that floats across the empty, dimly lit strip mall parking lot as I climb into the passenger's seat. "Let's go get this over and done with."

"I'm sorry about all this hassle."

"Don't be."

As we drive on to San Antonio Hospital I give everything I have to reassure my older sister that it's going to be ok, not to worry, this is nothing, we are all going to make it through. She turns to me and says, "Hey thanks for all your reassurances, but really shouldn't I be the one reassuring you here?"

*With both parents gone we have only one another now. Dennis is the baby. Loretta the oldest. I'm the proverbial middle-child. Sometimes it seems like we were born in the wrong order. Dennis seems the oldest (in spite of his penchant for sometimes breaking into a squawking chicken dance at family gatherings). He possesses all the trappings and traits you would expect an older sibling to possess—wife, children, house title— and is the one always reminding us to look both ways before crossing that metaphorical street. Loretta seems more the middle-child—widowed,*

*singlehandedly raising her daughter, the strong arching bridge connecting and keeping things together. And I play out my life out as if I were the youngest—still single, collecting comics, listening to Iggy Pop at volumes I probably shouldn't be, and constantly needing to be reminded to look both ways before crossing that street because you never know what might come hurtling towards you.*

"Now show me how high you can lift that left arm. You've been opened up quite a few times. Let's see what you can do."

You lift your left arm 4 inches and cringe.

"Is that as high as you can go?"

You nod. Your arm is so heavy it feels like it is made of solid concrete.

"Ok, now show me what you can do with the right arm."

You can't do a whole lot more with the right arm than you could with the left. It must have been made from the same batch of concrete.

It's not always going to be like this you tell yourself.

"Let's try lifting each arm one more time."

*It's not always going to be like this.*

You try to remember when it wasn't.

The emergency room waiting area at San Antonio is like every emergency room area I've ever been in. Anxious curtains of worry draped over everything. Till now I'd only ever been in an emergency waiting room as a concerned, worried visitor. They are sad uncomfortable places whether you are the one doing the worrying or the one who is being worried over.

I make my way down the list of questions in the clipboard in front of me and start making my circles. Circle Y for Yes. N for No. Alcohol Use? That's a Y. Regularly? Ok, ok you got me. That'd be another Y. Regular Exercise? A most definite N. I keep circling an endless parade of Ys and Ns regarding everything from irregular bloody bowel movements to genital warts. The process of filling out the form begins to feel less like standard paperwork and more like a sordid confession of my lapsed Catholic soul. I never knew how fortunate the simple act of circling the letter N could make a person feel.

Dennis comes rushing in and hugs me. A bright yellow T-shirt, a pair of worn beige corduroys, and a troubled smile adorn his thin frame.

"Aint this the shit?" he says, softly shaking his head.

"That it most definitely is."

Good old Pat is here too. Pat and I bonded twenty years ago at Chaffey Community College over Raymond Carver and Batman graphic novels. Pat is 6-foot-9 and jokes loud enough for the entire waiting room to hear, "This isn't about a weird venereal disease you may have contracted from some Pomona prostitute, is it?"

We both let out some nervous laughter.

What conversations can we strike up as we sit and wait and linger not really knowing? We talk about whether the Avengers movie coming out next month will be any good. Will the Hulk look more realistic than he did in that last Hulk movie? God, I hope so.

"An Avengers movie is almost upon us! Can you believe it?" Pat excitedly goes on. "We've been waiting our entire lives to see an Avengers movie! I wish my current self could go back in time and visit my 8-year-old self and tell him how one day there's going to be an actual honest-to-God friggin Avengers movie! You and I, old pal, are going to be catching that movie together come hell or highwater. We owe it to our former 8-year-old selves."

*The Avengers* broke all opening weekend box office records when it opened a few weeks back. Carlos and Liz graciously left a bootleg of it yesterday when they were here at Cedars-Sinai visiting. "We figured you probably hadn't gotten around to checking this out yet," Carlos lightly laughed, as he handed it to me.

I am 17 minutes into *The Avengers* when Pat enters the hospital room. His eyes widen as he glances at the iPad. "My God," he excitedly exclaims. "Is that an actual *Avengers* bootleg you're watching!?!"

"I can watch it later," I tell him. "I know you've already seen it."

Pat grabs a chair and scratches it across the floor towards the iPad's glowing screen.

"I told you I wasn't going to watch it without your ass. Remember?" Pat says. "Now turn the volume up a little, will ya?"

They finally call my name out across the San Antonio Emergency Room waiting area. They shake my hand. Have me confirm my name and birth date. Needles get stuck in. Blood gets drawn. Urine taken. It's well past midnight now. The good news is that the appendix will be staying where it is. The bad news is the blood sugar is 362. Looks like type 2 diabetes. They're going to keep me overnight for observation and to have someone come in tomorrow morning to go over diet restrictions and insulin injections with me.

It could always be worse.

"Your heart...it stopped beating...you were dead..."

The noises. The smells. The surroundings. It's weird waking up that first night at San Antonio. I'd never slept in a hospital bed before. I feel how Dorothy must have felt when she first landed in Oz. Stranger in a strange land. I wake up and it takes a minute to process and adjust to exactly where it is I am. I start taking inventory.

*It's so bright in here. What a night. What time is it? When can I leave?*

*Last night. I blacked out. That's right. Shit. Jen took me to Urgent Care. She's probably going nuts. I'd better text her. Let her know what's going on. Contact Dennis. Let work know…*

I text Jen: THEY KEPT ME OVERNIGHT AT SAN ANTONIO. NO WORRIES, OK? I THINK THE REAL REASON THEY ARE KEEPING ME OVERNIGHT IS BECAUSE OF HOW MUCH THEY JUST ADORE MY SENSE OF HUMOR.

Loretta is there at bedside. Her voice carries the carefully concerned tone that only an older sister's voice can carry as she asks me how I'm doing.

"I'm doing pretty alright…I think?"

"Really?"

"Well, I have had better days."

*…I have. Most definitely. But there have been far worse days. Days of loss and regret. This is not one of those. I will be out of here in a few hours and this will all be safely behind us. This day will soon take its place resting peacefully alongside all those other days that preceded it. It will be all but forgotten by next week.*

"Before we release you we need to make sure that you're comfortable with injecting yourself with insulin."

*Ok. Fair enough. Truth is, right now I'd inject myself with Coca-Cola and baking soda to get back to basking in the comforts of home.*

The nurse at San Antonio hands me a pamphlet on diabetes diet tips and a syringe.

"Now practice on the pillow for me," she instructs.

I successfully inject the small red pillow. It's a brave little pillow. It doesn't sweat. It doesn't wince. It doesn't bat an eye as the steel-tipped syringe digs in. And if it has some deep-seated neurotic fear of cold steel flesh-piercing needles it doesn't let it show. I wish I could say the same about myself as the nurse tells me "now go ahead and try it on yourself."

*I'm not afraid of ghosts. Or rollercoasters. Or flying. Sitting through the Texas Chainsaw Massacre while eating a bowl of chili wouldn't bother me. It's needles that freak me out.*

*Don't think about the needle. Think about anything but the needle. Think about strolling down a beach in slow motion with Jessica Alba in a blue bikini. Or a Radiohead song. Or strolling down the beach in slow motion with Jessica Alba in a blue bikini as she softly hums a Radiohead song into your ear...*

"I need you to focus and concentrate on what you're doing, Mr. Callaci."

"Ok, got it...no worries...no worries..." I tell her meekly.

*Good God this is going to be a bitch! If I didn't have to keep my eyes open to make sure I don't accidentally inject myself in the belly button I wouldn't. How come they can come up with a new iPhone every year but the damn needle hasn't evolved since the days of the wild frontier?*

It's not so bad. Really. Nothing I can't get used to. They give me a meter to read my blood sugar and start working on the paperwork for my release. It'll be an hour or so. Home. It'll be so good to be back there. To shower. Rest. Relax. Maybe watch some of those extras on the *Star Wars* blu-ray I'd been meaning to get to and then go and...

*Feeling dizzy...Is it me that's swaying or just everything around me?...this isn't good...this isn't good...*

I head to the small bathroom with the same sick shaky feeling I had the previous day before I blacked out. I don't pass out this time but feel I'm going to. Breathing isn't coming easy. Barely at all. It takes all I have to walk the few yards back to the hospital bed. By the time I reach the bed I am ready to collapse in on myself like a wet cardboard box.

...and then the small hospital room fills with Loretta's urgent voice calling out, "I'm getting someone **NOW!**"

## SOMETIMES IT SNOWS IN APRIL

"If you want to make God laugh, tell Him about your plans."

"Hey Jen, guess what I just did?"

"What'd you do this time?"

"I got us Springsteen tix! He'll be here in April. How exciting is that! Aren't you excited?"

"I am. I just won't be as excited as you are until April gets here. It's February. April is still a long ways off. And who knows what might happen between now and then?"

## April 2012

| M | T | W | T | F | S | S |
|---|---|---|---|---|---|---|
|   |   |   |   |   |   | 1 |
| 2 | 3 | 4 | 5 | 6 | 7 | 8 |
| 9 | 10 | 11 | 12 | 13 | 14 | 15 |
| 16 | 17 | 18<br>Check into Urgent Care/San Antonio Hospital | 19<br>Initial Heart Attack @San Antonio. Aorta balloon pump installed | 20<br>Heart stops beating momentarily when Aorta balloon pump tries to be removed | 21<br>~~L.A. Times Festival of Books~~<br>Angiogram | 22<br>~~L.A. Times Festival of Books~~<br>Quadruple Bypass |
| 23 | 24 | 25 | 26<br>~~Springsteen!!!~~<br>Tried to be taken off ventilator. Heart couldn't handle it– especially the right side | 27<br>Tried to be taken off ventilator again. Heart went into fatal rhythm.<br><br>ARBOR DAY | 28<br>Airlifted to Cedars-Sinai | 29 |
| 30 | 31 |   |   |   |   |   |

It's been close to 30 minutes of being stuck in neutral inside the Urgent Care waiting room being transferred from one Blue Cross operator to the next. 30 minutes, 1,800 seconds, and 1,800,000 milliseconds. Muzak versions of Celine Dion fill the eternal void between the transfers:

"Thank you for holding, Mr. Callaci. Let me transfer you to another representative who can better serve you."

A muzak version of Richard Marx's "Right Here Waiting" spews forth.

The irony is not lost on me.

Jen continues intensely gazing off into her phone as if she were wishing on a distant star.

I am spared the indignity of having to be exposed to the final chorus of Richard Marx's "Right Here Waiting" as I'm transferred to Darla, a woman with a strong Southern accent, who reunites me with my medical card number.

"Anything else I can do for you, hon?" Darla asks.

"I think I'm good."

When I look now at the photos taken that Easter it's obvious. I'm ashen. Not just a little tired or a little worn out. I'm ashen. How could I have not seen it? If my life had been a Springsteen song or Shakespearean sonnet I would have magnified and analyzed every last detail to death.

I never once considered that it might be more than middle-age that made tackling a large flight of stairs take several more breaths than it used to. I thought it was just work, grad school, and rock shows behind those late Sunday afternoon naps on the sofa.

*I still keep up. Long as I can still keep up. I am ok. I am ok. I am ok …*

This I believed.

And believed.

As hard as I could.

As long as I could.

Until I passed out across cold white linoleum bathroom tiles a few weeks after that Easter photo was taken.

It's Easter. I am at Dennis'. My 6-year-old nephew Henry is running around with a pair of felt bunny ears bouncing atop his blonde coiled curls.

"When are we going to look for eggs? I think we should go right now. Don't you, Uncle Allen?"

"Not right now, Henry. Not right now." Dennis interjects. "The egg hunt will happen a little later."

"Want to play Star Wars, Uncle Allen?"

"In a bit Henry. I'm just going to rest here on the sofa for a little bit. A little tired right now."

"How long is a little bit?"

"He'll play Star Wars with you a little later Henry, ok?" Dennis answers.

"Ok," Henry disappointedly says. "I've got some new figures you're really, really gonna like, Uncle Allen."

"I can't wait, Henry."

Henry's smile comes floating back.

My 17-year-old nephew Rael is plugged into his iPod trying his best to tune out another overbearing family festivity. Harmonie parades the floor in her Easter best and new glasses.

Loretta's laughter spills out the windows.

Dennis' wife Catherine calls out above Loretta's laughter for everyone to scrunch together on the sofa for an Easter family photo.

Henry doesn't really care to be part of the photo. He'd rather keep bouncing around in his bunny ears.

"Let's just do this. And do this now. Come on, people," Catherine pleads. It will only take a minute, she *promises* Henry.

"After the picture can we go look for eggs, mom?"

"We'll see."

The picture gets snapped.

"See, now that wasn't so bad? Was it?" she asks Henry.

Henry doesn't answer. He has already fled the photo shoot with his fuzzy bunny ears in tow to grab his Easter basket.

"You sure you feeling alright there, little brother?" Loretta asks me as Henry races off. "You're looking a little worn."

"I guess I am a little worn. Grad school, work, teaching…"

"You got to remember to be good to yourself."

"I will."

"Promise?"

"Promise."

*"I was so terrified to see you that first time. I didn't know what to expect. I was getting all the text updates on my phone and pictured you so frail and weak with all these tubes and IVs and…I was scared…scared you'd feel how scared I was and you'd get that scared too…"*

"I had to come," Karol says clutching a stuffed bear in a baseball uniform as she enters the narrow San Antonio Hospital room with her sister Isabel. "It's from my mom," she says glancing down at the bear in the game day fatigues she holds in her hands. Karol presses down on the bear's stomach and a rusted music box version of "Take Me Out to the Ballgame" bursts out from the bear's belly.

"I don't care if I never get back," I sing wildly off-key in a vain attempt to spring a smile from Karol's worried face.

Karol and I have known each other forever. Not only did I introduce her to her husband Bob but I also ended up being the second drunkest groomsman on their rain-soaked wedding day. She has reminded me several times over the years of both of these milestones.

She looks down at me lying there in the narrow San Antonio

Hospital room bed and clutches the stuffed bear a bit tighter. "I'm sorry," she says. "I told myself I wasn't going to cry when I saw you but I am."

Her tears form.

"It's only type 2 diabetes," I say. "Just like Isabel was diagnosed with earlier this year. Nothing that can't be dealt with. Look at how well Isabel is doing. No tears, ok? They're getting all the paperwork together right now to release me in just a few hours. Watch out, America I'm going to be out there dancing in no time …"

Her tears keep coming.

*Karol will tell me months later how hard she tried to keep from crying that afternoon but there was this overwhelming feeling inside of her that she just couldn't shake telling her that this was more than type 2 diabetes.*

*… It was the exact same feeling she felt right before learning of her father's passing.*

I press the bear's belly hoping one more inspired version of "Take Me Out to the Ballgame" will make Karol's tears go away.

It doesn't.

"Your brother is in severe critical condition. He most likely could not survive a bypass surgery. A heart transplant is the last and the only hope he has. An intra-Aortic Balloon Pump will be placed inside him to help his heart pumping until surgery can be done. You can meet with the surgeon, Dr. Wang, in the morning."

"Do you really need to use all that butter?" asks the girl he met recently through the library's sci-fi book club. Her voice floats above the din of the hustling waitresses, bustling busboys and the strains of Thelonious Monk that serve as the soundtrack to the dimly lit college town bar.

She wears a soft tan dress. Her eyes are a few shades darker, a few degrees warmer, than the dress. It's the first time he has seen her wear contacts instead of glasses.

As for him?

… well, his shirt is tucked in. His glasses have been recently Windexed. And both socks match.

"I don't know if I've ever seen a slice of bread bathed in so much butter," she tells him.

"How'd you expect a guy you recently met in a sci-fi book club to eat?" he blurts defensively.

"How'd you expect a girl you recently met in a sci-fi club to react to all that butter?"

"I don't know…I'd expect a girl I met in a sci-fi club to be pretty low maintenance, Jen."

"Pretty low maintenance? Me? You have no idea, do you?" she gently laughs. "Now scrape half that butter off that bread or trouble's sure to follow."

The staff is gathered around the x-ray screen at San Antonio Community Hospital watching your blood flow. The coronary angiogram is in progress. A contrast dye has been injected into your arteries through a thin plastic tube to help them monitor the blood circulation. The angiogram captures what the EKG does not. It shows the blood to be circulating about as smoothly as rush hour traffic after a nine car pile-up.

There is so much blockage there might not be much more they can do.

"Call his brother and sister in," orders Dr. Wang. "***Immediately…***"

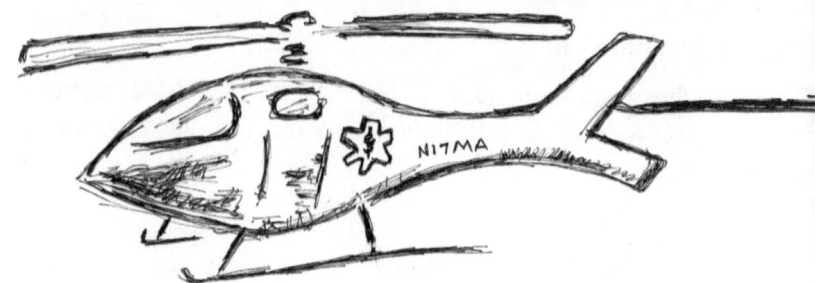

**The quadruple bypass surgery traffic report**
His ECG shows the heart pumping at a mere 20%. The RCA (Right Coronary Artery) and LAD (Left Anterior Descending) are both 100% blocked. The circumflex branch of the left coronary artery is underdeveloped, probably from birth (5% of population are diagnosed with this). Three of four arteries are completely blocked and not functioning. They will be pulling a small length of the saphenous vein from his leg and attaching it to the blocked artery. The vein will be attached at both ends of the four clotted portions to create a 'bypass' for the blood to reach the heart...the great saphenous vein is the largest artery in the human body extending from the top of the foot to the upper thigh and groin ...

"God damn I hate texting," Dennis says, clutching my scratch covered cellphone with the worn-down keypad. "I swear to God I am never going to own one of these damn things," he grumbles as he hits send and tosses out another text message.

>>Dr. Wang from San Antonio just gave Allen better odds to make it through the bypass surgery than the cardiologist did yesterday but there is a long list of potential risks.
>>Allen came through the quadruple bypass with no complications.
>>After recovering well for the last 3 or 4 days Allen just had an episode and is unstable. His heart went into a fatal rhythm when they took out the aortic balloon pump. They had to shock his heart and put him back on the pump and ventilator. They are working on putting the pump back in and the ventilator. Pls don't come just Pray and we will update as soon as we know more xo
>>Dr. Wang told us Allen's only chance is a heart transplant due to

 the weakness of his heart. He will be airlifted by helicopter to Cedars-Sinai tomorrow morning.

You're heavily sedated as they roll you towards the copter. But not sedated enough. You feel the sun hitting. Your eyes are partially open. Your mind a barely conscious fog. You shut your eyes to prevent being blinded by the sun. Closing your eyes helps some but you still feel the roast of the rays beating down on you. You're not exactly sure where you're going or why. Only that you're going.

My stepsister Chris remembers it like this:

*"Walking through the hallway following the gurney to the helicopter - I think I was holding Loretta up - like we were all walking along on air. I was happy and hopeful that they were taking you to Cedars. Loretta and Dennis told me later it wasn't like that for them at all - it was more like your life flashing before them."*

They are pushing forward. It's a military operation. Each step has been carefully calculated and coordinated as they slowly roll you out across the asphalt battlefield towards the tarmac. They reach their hands across you to shield you from the sun, as they march you and the battalion of equipment you're attached to steadily and bumpily forward. There is the sound of blades coming from above, slicing through the hot afternoon air. They gently lift you in.

Once inside the copter, the sun now off your face, you half-way open your eyes again.

"My God he's still conscious," a voice above you cries.

"How can that be?" cries another.

There's less than a 25% chance you'll survive the flight and make it to Cedars-Sinai alive.

The copter lifts off.

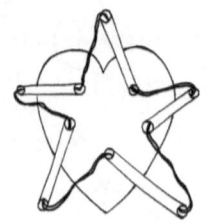

# ER TO THE STARS

"Turn to the Stars When You're Grey" - Refrigerator

You're the last person anyone would expect to find at Cedars-Sinai—the aptly nicknamed "ER to the Stars." Madonna had hernia surgery here. Paul Stanley came here for heart palpitations. David Hasselhoff was famously brought here to detox after being captured on video by his daughter shirtless and drunkenly slurring his way through a greasy cheeseburger.

You're no international sex symbol/pop icon.

You're not Paul Stanley.

You're not even David Hasselhoff.

You are a librarian, professor, and singer of a band named after a kitchen appliance. You are from the Inland Empire. If Beverly Hills is the glitz and glamour center of the universe, the Inland Empire is the region farthest away. The Inland Empire is derisively referred to as the "Land of the Dirt People" by a local Los Angeles radio station. A land of interchangeable pastel painted strip malls, freshly built two-car garage gated housing tracts and faded ashtray-smelling apartment complexes left over from the late '60s with names such as the Oasis and Paradise.

You've always believed that people end up where it is they need to be at a certain time for a certain reason. It might only be in hindsight that you realize why it was that you were at a certain place, surrounded by a certain circle at a certain time but eventually it all becomes clear.

The "Land of the Dirt People" lies just within the 60 mile radius that was required for you to be sent to the ER to the Stars.

You've been sleeping like Michael Jackson. At least you were. The IV loaded with Propofol has been shut off. You might not think you've heard of Propofol before, but you have. It is the sleep inducing anesthetic Michael Jackson had been on when they found his body.

Propofol is so potent that it is critical to have a medical professional standing by at all times when it is administered to a patient in case he should stop breathing. They have to shut off the Propofol IV drip for short periods several times a day to make sure you're still in there.

The Propofol leaves your system within 30 seconds of being shut off and leaves you hazily conscious.

They call Dennis, Loretta, and your loved ones in whenever they shut off the Propofol so they can see you in a somewhat conscious state.

The way that turning off the Propofol would instantly animate you and turning it back on would instantly silence you reminded Loretta of a puppeteer manipulating a puppet.

You hear a voice asking if you can wiggle your toes for her. Move your fingers. Open your eyes.

You think you hear her say "That's good."

And then the Propofol comes racing back.

If we shadows have offended,
Think but this, and all is mended,
That you have but slumber'd here
While these visions did appear.
And this weak and idle theme,
No more yielding, but a dream.
-William Shakespeare. *A Midsummer Night's Dream. Act V, Scene I*

```
My Complete Unabridged Collection of Memories
-April 29-May 6 2012:
```

A voice drifts above your silent, heavily sedated body.

"I know you. I know you're still in there. I know you can hear me."

It's Karol.

"We are all right here for you. We have been right here. We have tried to remain strong. Now we need you to be strong. We need you to keep pushing. We need you to pull yourself through all this and be right here for us."

Make a fist.

The only sounds in the small Cedars-Sinai hospital room are CNN and the machines and monitors encircling you which are cawing off-key like a flock of nervous crows.

MAKE A FIST.

Your arms are so thin you could wrap two fingers around your elbow. Your fingers move in pained slow motion as you try to clench them together. The CNN crawl coming from the television hoisted in the corner above you shows Obama leading Romney by 4 percentage points if the election were held today. You bite your lip, grind your teeth and try to complete the monumental task of trying to clench your fingers together.

**MAKE A FIST.**

Only a few more inches till thumb touches fingers.

Shit!

The fingers snap back into place.

The thumb stays right where it is.

Almostalmostalmostalmostalmost

Again.

Make a fist …

### Cedars-Sinai Intensive Care Unit (ICU) Visitor Policy

- Visitors must be 18 years or older.
- Visitors are permitted 24 hours a day.
- One person at a time is allowed for five minutes every hour
- Call from the lobby on the ICU phone before you come to the unit, to make sure you are not interrupting patient care procedures.
- Tea and coffee are available in the ICU waiting areas.
- Food is not allowed in the ICU waiting areas.
- Volunteers in the waiting areas will take messages for you if you leave the waiting area.
- Children under the age of 12 are not permitted in the patient's room.

*They drive all those miles to see me and most of the time I'm either completely under or so completely out of it I am barely able to acknowledge their presence. I know you're there...don't leave...I'm tired and worn but I feel you there ...*

*... I feel you there...softly humming a Beatles song to yourself... making sure to keep your humming lower than the noisy grind of the respirator...quietly turning a page on a book of Sudoku puzzles...trying not to laugh too loudly at something or other...not too long from now you will no longer be sitting in that chair worriedly flipping through old People magazines...and I will no longer be hooked up in this bed...and we will sing "Eleanor Rigby" together...and I will help you finish up that Sudoko puzzle...and you can tell me exactly what it was that made you laugh the way you did that day...*

"Maybe I should read you some *Twilight*. It might be my only chance," Jen says softly. She's not sure if you'll even hear her in your current half-conscious state. She says it to help fill the worried quiet that coats the small hospital room like a thin layer of paint.

The conversations you and Jen have had over the years regarding *Twilight* have always gone something like this:

"Vampires aren't supposed to sparkle, Jen. They are the bloodthirsty undead. And even if there were vampires who sparkled, they would not fall madly in love with whiny, self pitying, self-obsessed 17-year-old girls."

"I don't care what you say, Mr. English Major," she'd retort. "I love my *Twilight*. And I love my Edward."

You don't have either the voice or the strength to give her your usual deconstruction of *Twilight* as you lie almost motionless in the hospital bed. You have only your eyes to convey the depth of your disdain for poorly executed sparkling vampire epics.

She is surprised at this scornful look of literary contempt, but not really. In fact it actually makes her want to laugh. It's the first time she's wanted to laugh in awhile. She's been a mess at work. Crying when no one is looking. Arguing and yelling when anyone is.

*I met Jen about 5 years ago when she attended a sci-fi book club meeting I help run at the library. I know a beautiful, dynamic headstrong woman appearing at a Rancho Cucamonga library sci-fi book club meeting sounds more fantastic and improbable than anything to be found in the collected works of Ray Bradbury, H.G. Wells, and Jules Verne combined but that really is how we met.*

"Don't worry," she softly smiles. "We'll read some *Game of Thrones* instead."

She begins to quietly read aloud. Your eyes begin slowly slipping shut to the sound of her voice.

*Oh shit,* she thinks as she reaches a steamy sex scene. *I can't read this part out loud in a hospital room. Knowing my luck one of the nurses will walk in right now and think I'm some kind of raging pervert. He's out for the night anyway. I'm going to stop.*

You take your two frail hands as high as they can go and make the international sign for her to keep reading, keep reading, keep reading.

And for the second time in a long-ass while she feels like laughing.

# THUNDER ON THE THRESHOLD OF DEATH

*THUNDER ON THE THRESHOLD OF DEATH the cover promises.*

*Thor and The Thing are surrounded by Seth "the Lord of the Unliving" and his skeletal army of the undead.*

*"Battle as never before Ben Grimm…for Earth and Asgard hang in the balance," Thor calls out to The Ever-Lovin' Blue-Eyed Thing.*

*The sunbeams crawl across the alleys and cul-de-sacs before finally cutting through a bedroom window towards a crumpled bottom bunk bed. The sounds of weekend suburbia abound. The low buzz of lawnmowers, the machine gun spitfire of front yard sprinklers, the squeal of a breeze kicking through a rusty swing set, and the quick, incessant parental knocking on an 11-year-old boy's bedroom door.*

"It's a beautiful Saturday afternoon," my mom calls through the door. "You need to put down that comic and go outside. Get some sun. Be active. That's what kids your age need to be doing."

"But it's The Thing and it's Thor and they're together…and they're battling Seth the Lord of the Undead…and …"

"The Lord of the Undead's first name is Seth?… honestly Allen John…

*If you spent half as much time exercising as you do reading those comics I bet you'd be replacing Bruce Jenner on the Wheaties box ..."*

"... awwww man... Can't I at least finish reading 'Thunder on the Threshold of Death' first?"

"Not right now."

"I bet dad would let me finish reading it."

"Your father won't be here to pick you up until tomorrow," she says taking an exasperated drag from her cigarette. "Now put that comic down Allen John and go outside. There'll be plenty of time for 'Thunder on the Threshold of Death' later ..."

You were not there. Your body was there but you no longer were. Eyes so swollen the eyelids have flipped up. Face so bloated. Opened and reopened. All Dr. Ramzy can tell your family is that they've done all it is they can. It's up to you now.

You've lost so much blood. They hover desperately above, squeezing the plastic bags of bright red liquid back into you as fast as they can.

The RVAD—a mechanical pump designed to support heart function and blood flow—isn't taking like they'd hoped it would. If it doesn't take it's going to be a far more difficult conversation Dr. Ramzy will be having with your family.

You'd rather not write anything more about that time. There are things that are too immense to be lifted, to be looked at completely all at once, to ever be properly weighed and inventoried.

You'd rather write about catching Neil Young at the Hollywood Bowl instead.

A brisk October evening at the Hollywood Bowl. I am there

with Dennis, Catherine and Rael. Longtime Refrigerator cover artist extraordinaire Amy is here too. She is praying in vain that Neil will open with "Change Your Mind." He doesn't. He opens his set with a feedback soaked version of "Love and Only Love." And it's perfect. There I am at my favorite venue, listening to a favorite artist, with my favorite people.

A bright white cross shines from the hill above. The hard wooden benches are no more comfortable than the well-worn church pews at St Joseph's. I feel like I will be asked to rise and receive communion any second now.

The Hollywood sign glistens in the northern distance. A different glow than the one I have recently known. The one I would see from behind thick-plated glass on my daily walks at Cedars-Sinai with a holiday parade of life assist devices attached to my side. The Hollywood sign would beckon to me then like a lighthouse calling a lost ship to shore. *So close and so far.*

Tonight the sign glows from above like a favorite Christmas ornament. The path of this universe does not run straight. The path of this universe is filled with sharp turns and unexpected detours. The path of this universe is unmapped but leads eventually to where it is you are meant to be.

Amy offers a sip of her warm overpriced beer. I happily take her up on her offer. As the quick sip rolls its way down my throat I look up and around.

At the stars.

Family.

Friends.

I'm here.

I'm still here.

Faith does not abandon you in your darkest hours, it sustains you.

"The RVAD surgery was successful. But he has been on the life support machines for such an extended period that some neurological damage may have occurred. There could be brain damage. There is no way of knowing until he regains full consciousness" the Dr. gravely tells Dennis and Loretta. "When he finally comes to, he might not be the brother you've always known anymore."

I've changed. I used to be so patient. I did not create waves. I quietly rode them out. I've become a loud breaking tide since returning home. My story arc should begin with an impatient soul who is angered and frustrated with the universe and his place in it. It should end with that same soul being redeemed and acquiring a profound acceptance for all of humanity. It shouldn't be the other way around.

I visited Pat's wife Lisa last night. She was home recovering from a kidney/bladder infection that had sent her to the hospital twice. She had to go back the second time due to dehydration. Her kidneys have been weak since she was a child. She loves her Pepsi even if her kidneys don't. It is her kryptonite. Picking up a 64 oz Big Gulp on her commute to work is a morning norm. It's not just artificially sweetened citric acid to her, it's a childhood connection to her father. She's a sentimentalist. It had taken her more than a decade to part with the electric can opener I had given her and Pat as a wedding gift.

I had never raised my voice to her before, during, or after giving her that can opener until last night.

"What is this?" I said, pulling a Pepsi can out by its throat from her fridge. "You told me you were done putting this crap inside yourself due to all your health issues."

"I don't smoke…or do drugs…or abuse alcohol…it's just this one thing."

"…and all it takes is this ONE thing to put you on dialysis. Is that what you want? Because that's where this is leading. What's it going to be? This can? Or your future? You know what's inside this can? The devil's urine!"

*Good God, I sound worse than Jen.*

"You don't understand," she pleads helplessly as the Pepsi spirals its way down the gurgling drain.

"You're right. I don't," I answer crunching the empty can and violently tossing it into the small plastic waste bucket beneath the sink.

"I appreciate all you're saying. And I agree," she says in a shaken voice. "You just don't…don't understand how hard it is to stop."

"Really? I don't understand sacrifice? Want me to fax you a list of everything I've given up these past few months?" I shout, tearing another can open and pouring its carbonated contents down the drain. "Let's compare lists."

"I know. I'm sorry…" she says hanging her head toward the freshly vacuumed carpeting. "I guess I can't be playing that card with you can I?…I'm trying Al…I am…I just don't know what to do…I don't have the same kind of resolve in me that you do."

"Once you stop thinking like that you will."

"I'm gonna try, Al," she answers with her eyes still locked in on the freshly vacuumed carpet. "That's all I have. That's all I can tell you. You've really become Mr. Health Awareness 2012, haven't you?…maybe we all need to start addressing you as Dr. Callaci instead of Professor Callaci."

## A Teachable Moment

### Presented February 2012 at Mt San Antonio Community College Bldg 26A-Rm 211 by Professor Callaci

"Your ultimate reward in this class won't be measured by the simple letter grade you receive when this semester concludes. It will be measured by how much you learn, grow and take with you by the time June arrives. That's what I want you to remember most as this semester progresses. Real growth and real learning come from battling and struggling and ultimately transcending."

FUCK!

I CAN'T BREATHE!

## I CAN'T BREATHE!

The plastic tube wraps its way from the ventilator it's attached to past your vocal cords and down into your lungs like one of the facehuggers from *Alien*. You want to reflexively rip the endotracheal tube right out of your throat but your hands have been tied down and you've been partially sedated for this very reason.

You've never despised anything in your life the way you despise this tube.

Not war.

Poverty.

Or Greedo shooting first instead of Han Solo in the *Star Wars: Episode IV - A New Hope* special edition.

If you could speak you might note the irony of how much you've come to despise the very thing that has been keeping you alive the past week and a half since you were helicoptered in.

… But you can't speak.

Or drink.

Or breathe on your own.

There is not a whole lot you can really do except give the nurses a shaky nod when they ask if you would like them to apply some more wet swabs to your chapped dry desert of a mouth.

You're reminded of the violent, crashing scream of the Santa Ana winds as they suction out some more mucus from your lungs. Suction is needed 3-4 times an hour to keep the lungs clear. You do your best to muster the strength to let out a few painful ratty coughs to contribute your part to the mucus removal cacophony.

"Just breathe and relax. Breathe and relax. I need you to breathe deeply and relax for me," Nurse Anna tells you. "In a few minutes I'll be taking the tube out. Work with me. Breathe."

You hear her.

*Breathe deep and relax.*

You're trying.

*Breathe deep and relax.*

You feel like you're drowning.

# AIR

## AIR

### AIR

You've got to come up for air. You feel like you're breathing through a broken straw. *Slow deep breaths. Slow deep breaths. Close your eyes. Focus on the ceiling. Not on where you are. Not on the tube. Not on your goatee covered in dried saliva.* You've got to do it. Ok, ok. You're going to do this. A few more minutes. Just a few more minutes, she said, before they remove it.

For those who might wonder what this all must feel like imagine chewing tinfoil while being buried neck-deep in dry ice and multiply that by 10.

# AIR

## AIR

### AIR

One minute you're there at your desk planning a graduation for the library's tutoring program, wrangling stormtroopers for Star Wars day, and daydreaming about an upcoming Springsteen show and the next minute YOU ARE HERE. Gasping and thrashing for air like a goldfish on the sidewalk.

Stepsister Chris is holding your hand. Looking down on you. Comforting you. "Can't you just take it out now…what do a few more minutes matter?" she calls out to Nurse Anna. "He's suffering." You squeeze Chris' hand even tighter in support and agreement. Your face is as red as your eyes are puffed out and watery. The strain has been so great that you've popped a blood vessel.

"This is going to hurt but it's going to be quick," Nurse Anna says. It feels like sandpaper as the tube is slowly pulled and works its way up your throat and out your body. It could feel like a dozen rusty razors and you wouldn't mind. You just want it gone.

And then it is gone.

Gone.

A deep breath.

And then another.

And another.

And another.

## AIR

A single tear of infinite relief scrolls down your face. You lack the strength to lift up either arm to wipe it away. The sole tear rolls its way down as Nurse Anna tells you that she will need you to take deep breaths and cough every few hours over the next several days.

"This is going to be painful," she tells you. "Your throat is as raw and tender right now as it is sore, but it's important you do this. You have to do this in order to keep mucus from collecting in your lungs and catching pneumonia. You understand?"

You nod to Nurse Anna. The solitary tear has finished its run from your face and hit the pillow without a sound. The room goes silent for a second. You've got no voice but grab Chris' hand again and try to gargle out the word "thanks" from your bruised, battered throat as best you can.

You hope she hears you.

## SONGS IN THE KEY OF LIFE

"He is sick. Really sick," the doctor tells them. "His heart function right now is less than 20%. Two blocked arteries. A valve defect from birth. This is serious. This isn't good and hasn't been good for a long while. How active has his life been the past few years? I can't imagine it's been a very active one. Climbing a small flight of stairs must have been a challenge with the heart he has in him now."

Dennis and Loretta let the doctor know that not only have you climbed a fair amount of stairs the past few years you've also been working full-time at a library, teaching an English class at the local community college, and singing in a rock band.

The doctor is taken aback, a little amazed, to hear of the life you've been leading. It doesn't seem possible given the weak engine you've got pumping inside of you.

I imagine the part that took the doctor aback the most was the part about being a singer. I look like a librarian. An English Professor. Not a rock 'n' roll singer. 5-foot-3…glasses…goatee…and a brown and graying patch of short curly hair that matches the goatee.

No one has ever mistaken me for Mick Jagger (see chart).

| Category | Mick Jagger | Me |
|---|---|---|
| Knighted by Queen of England | Yes | As of this writing "no." |
| Supermodels Romantically Linked With | 17 | 0 |
| Familiar with Dewey Decimal System | ? | YES |
| Persistent Rumors of Having Once Slept With David Bowie | Yes | No |

"Tell Uncle Allen he can borrow my CD player for as long as he needs it."

Dennis tells you how Henry said that as he carried the small plastic Fisher-Price CD player out of his bedroom and headed to the hospital. Henry's CD player is one of his prized possessions. The White Stripes. The Ramones. Black Sabbath. His musical knowledge and taste is impressive for a 7-year-old (or even a 17-year-old).

You turn your head slowly in the direction of the small plastic CD player. You close your eyes and hear an echo of Henry's voice saying "Tell Uncle Allen he can borrow my CD player for as long as he needs it."

You mist up. Smile. And mist up again.

*Music is where I've always gone to heal. I was 7 when my parents divorced. And it was "Someone Saved My Life Tonight" by Elton John* that helped hold me together through their separation. When I was a small, scrawny, glasses wearing, acne covered, retainer fitted Junior High schooler, I lost myself in KISS. Where else was I going to go? After KISS came Quadrophenia by The Who.

You have no voice only two thin shaky arms and ten warbling fingers to communicate with. You motion to Dennis. You make a slow, trembling motion mimicking the turning of a radio dial.

"You need more ice chips?" Dennis asks trying to decipher your pantomimed code.

You shake your head "no" and make the motion again.

"Ok, ok...let's try this again...You need me to go get the nurse?" Dennis guesses.

You begin to feel like a squeaking, bobbing dolphin trying to communicate with its trainer.

You shake your head "no" again and point a finger to the white plastic Fisher-Price CD player.

"Ahhhh...I think I got you now!" Dennis exclaims looking over at the plastic CD player.

He goes to the player. He grabs *Quadrophenia* by The Who out of the stack of CDs he had brought along with the player. "What about this?"

You enthusiastically nod three times in the affirmative.

He throws the disc in.

*Quadrophenia*. It had been the soundtrack to your awkward adolescence. It was everything that you were at the time. Angry. Confused. Alienated. You connected with it intensely. It made you feel a lot less alone and a little more ok than you would have felt otherwise. For you it felt closer to a rite of passage than a song cycle. It feels like that again as Dennis presses play and *Quadrophenia* echoes, aches and rages from Henry's small white plastic Fisher Price player.

You close your eyes. You are weak but feel yourself moving to the rhythm. You can't really speak but find yourself squeaking along with the words as best you can. Grinding your teeth. Clenching your weakened fists as best you can. Closing your tired eyes a little tighter. You know this song. You were this song. You are this song. Sing it… sing it…sing it.

…and so you sing …

To the world outside it may sound like a forced breathless whisper.

But this is not a whisper.

It is a roar.

Love, Reign O'er Me.

```
From: dennis callaci
Re: first few pages
Sent: Monday, December 17, 2012 9:18 PM
```
Allen,
It was draining to read but I'm so proud of you for having the strength to put it all down. I had to stop reading more than a couple times. It cut like a gentle knife. It brought back a lot of things I'd rather not have brought back.
When the cardiologist told us you had 4 days to live at San Antonio he followed it up with "Pull it together, you are going to see your brother in 5 minutes and you need to be positive." I stepped out of the waiting room, then walked backed in and to no one in particular (though Loretta and stepsister Chris were in the room), I said aloud "No, I do not accept this." I remember moving my hand in a motion you make when you are erasing a chalkboard and it was all slow motion out of body. God, I really don't want to revisit those scary times. It was the worst night of my life.
Love you
-Dennis

You've got so many questions regarding those days you spent unconscious, opened up, sedated and desperately hanging from invisible silken threads. It's odd to think that there are days of your life that you will never have a single memory of. Like your life is a movie with missing scenes that were shot but have now been lost forever.

The voice of a 6-year-old girl fills in the darkness.

"All the time everywhere everything's hearts are beating and squirting and talking to each other in ways I can't understand."

It is early August. It has been roughly two weeks since I've been cleared to go to see movies at a walk-in theater. I've been indulging on film like a man who hasn't eaten in a week might indulge at an all you can eat buffet. Today's film is *Beasts of the Southern Wild*. It's about a 6-year-old girl adapting and surviving after a devastating natural disaster and how she braves on. It's about cutting across and making it through the storms you were vaguely aware of but not fully prepared for.

I self-consciously wait for the theater houselights to dim before pulling the surgical mask over my face. A lot of the self-loathing feelings I acquired from having to wear my dental headgear in 4th grade and being taunted in the halls with "hey harmonica head" rustle from within. And then, another voice surfaces from within to drown it out. The voice sounds like the husky Sicilian baritone of my 90-year-old cigar smoking Uncle Joe:

*For God's sake just put on the mask already. Who the hell you trying to be here? Mr. Universe? Who gives a good god damn?*

The mask goes on.

"The whole universe depends on everything fitting together just right," the young girl's voice coming off the silver screen continues on. "If you can fix the broken pieces everything can get right back…

bust even the smallest piece, the whole universe will get busted."

Dennis was at the movies the night I got sick. He came home to a small post-it stuck on the fridge by Catherine that read "Harmonie is sleeping, talk to me."

He still has that small faded post-it.

# BROTHER LOVE'S TRAVELLING SALVATION SHOW

"Hello brother."

"Hello brother," I respond warmly back to the thin, twenty-something Asian kid. He could easily pass for one of the students in my class at Mt. SAC. He is obviously not my brother. Except for the scratchy egg yolk colored surgical masks that cover the bottom half of our faces we look nothing alike.

Jason's transplant and mine happened mere hours apart. As mine happened after his, he has taken to calling me "little brother." He does this in spite of the fact that I have two decades on him easy. I wonder how disorienting it must be to the rest of the people here in the waiting room to hear a young Asian kid loudly referring to a middle-aged white guy as his "little brother."

*In a parallel universe he could have been one of my students. And people say I'm way too young to have had this shit happen. He probably gets carded trying to buy a ticket to go see* Hangover *sequels at the local multiplex.*

Jason's sister, like mine, patiently tends to his side as he waits to get called back.

You can scour the small waiting room and get a pretty good read on how far along everyone is in the recovery process. We newbies are easy to spot. We are the ones in the French's mustard colored surgical masks. We are the ones with the immune systems still so vulnerable that our surgical masks are not to be taken off until we reach the parking lot. The ones who will be coming to clinic twice a week for the next month to monitor and make sure the new heart is not being rejected by its new host. The struggle is still fresh in our eyes. Our staples are still protruding. Our scars are still puffy and sensitive to the touch. Our walkers are still glued to our side like a faithful Labrador Retriever. For us the mental processing is just beginning. *What happened? What happens next? What happens tomorrow?*

"Mr. Callaci, you can come back now to get the blood drawn," the nurse calls out.

"Good luck, little brother," Jason muffles from behind his mask.

"You too, brother." I muffle back from behind mine.

I'm sure there is a better world out there somewhere. A world where it rains flying unicorns. The laundry washes itself. And the potassium pills are smaller than baby aspirin and taste just like pears. But that world is not this one.

"Awwwwwwwwkkkk," I gag like a broken foghorn as the Grinch-green potassium pill shoots out of my throat like a drenched cannonball.

"I know it's rough," Nurse Merlinda tells me as I indiscreetly try and pick the slippery, saliva-covered potassium pill I have just spit up like a geyser for the third time from the front of my water-logged gown.

The potassium pills are larger than a pregnant horsefly. My gag reflex is as sensitive as an infant's rash. The potassium pills go down like oblong capsules of self-strangulation. Swallowing the potassium pill seems like an impossible task. Like sculpting a life-size replica of Mount Rushmore out of Jell-O or devouring a giraffe in less than three bites.

"I know honey. I know," Merlinda says sympathetically as I look down at the spit-soaked potassium pill I hold between my fingers with helpless frustration. "Let's try a different approach. Do you like applesauce?"

I nod.

Merlinda is kind enough to have the potassium pills grounded into a powder and mixed in with some applesauce. How does it taste? Let's just say the Food Network will not be educating its viewers on how to mix applesauce with potassium pills for that "perfect holiday meal taste explosion" any time soon.

The mixture gives the applesauce the delicate texture of beach sand.

She was in love with the idea of living less than 20 minutes away from the crashing waves and squawking seagulls even if she couldn't get there as much as she'd like. She'd lived within earshot of the roar and whisper of the waves for two decades. If you were to ask her what kind of person she was she would instinctively tell you she was a "beach person."

Despite her longstanding love for the sea and sand she, and her daughter, moved away from it in late summer 2011 to the inland suburb where both her brothers lived. There had been a feeling pulling her there like the strongest of tides. A feeling telling her this was where she needed to be. Close to family in case, God forbid, anything should happen.

Pat texts Loretta from across the San Antonio Community Hospital Maternity Ward border. LORETTA. AT SAN ANTONIO NOW. SNUCK MY WAY THROUGH. EVERYTHING SEEMS ALRIGHT. THEY HAVE MOVED AL TO THE CARDIO WARD.

How a guy 6 feet 9 inches tall with a voice that carries like a foghorn managed to make it inside San Antonio Hospital undetected after visiting hours I can't pretend to understand. Pat still claims to this day that it was by "covertly" cutting through the hospital's maternity ward. An image that always evokes a smile. In the two decades I've known Pat I've known him to be as "covert" as a chainsaw buzzing behind a gospel choir.

CARDIO WARD? WHAT DO YOU MEAN CARDIO WARD? Loretta frantically texts Pat back. THEY WERE SAYING IT WAS HIS APPENDIX ONLY HOURS AGO AT URGENT CARE.

She waits 10 minutes. And then another 10. She gets no response back from Pat. It's well beyond midnight now. Dennis and Catherine are taking care of Harmonie. *Cardio ward? If Pat can sneak himself in there, I know I surely can,* she says to herself and grabs her car keys.

She is numb to the song spilling from the car stereo as she races her way back to San Antonio Community Hospital.

*Your mom is singing along to Neil Diamond's "Sweet Caroline" as she scrambles up some Sunday morning eggs. Neil Diamond's* Love at the Greek *is your soundtrack for 1977. Not because you necessarily like Neil Diamond but because your mom loves him. The sounds of "Cracklin' Rosie" and "Brother Love's Travelling Salvation Show" are the only sounds the bulky stereo in the living room, which resembles the monolith*

*from Kubrick's 2001 turned on its side.*

"It'd be so wonderful to see him live one day. Wouldn't it?" she says to no one in particular, before getting back to battering the eggs with a plastic spatula to the beat of "Sweet Caroline."

"You absolutely won't believe this," stepsister Chris says. "So there I am having lunch at Jerry's Deli and it turns out the guy in the booth behind me is Neil Diamond. Can you even believe it?"

"My mom was a huge fan. She would have gotten the biggest kick out of that," I manage to cough out from the back of my still aching throat.

"I didn't even know he was there until I was leaving and the waiter happened to tell me. Says he comes in all the time. Probably better I didn't know until I was leaving. I might have been tempted to bug the poor guy for an autograph when all he wanted was a quiet cup of coffee. Did you hear that Elton John is here at Cedars too? I heard that just the other day. Looks like the musical spirits are everywhere."

"Musical spirits and spirits in general," I add.

My mom, the Neil Diamond fan, had passed away four years earlier.

"Hey I seemed to have misplaced your mom's phone number. Can you text that over to me real quick," I text Jen.

"Nice try," she responds.

Getting Jen's mom's phone number is a long running gag between the two of us. "The last thing I need is for the two of you to be talking," comes her stock answer.

"Can you imagine the reports I'd be sending back to her regarding her daughter?"

"I can," she laughs. 'That's why you ain't EVER getting each other's number."

*Allen. This is Jennifer's mother, Suzanne. Giving you a call. Leaving you a message. I just wanted to reach out...to send you my love...I'm really...just really concerned...maybe I need to come out there...just to be there...to help out...please just give me a call...let me know...*

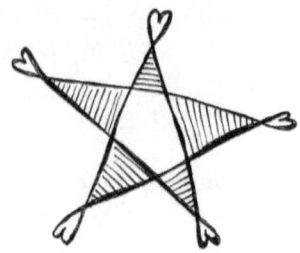

## LIKE A BALLOON WITHOUT A STRING

The visit at City of Hope has been as crisp as the windless Autumn morning. I've been meaning to drop in since September. Next week will be Thanksgiving. The morning visit overflows with gracious people who have never seen me telling me how happy they are to see me.

"This was nice," I tell Jen as I hug her goodbye. "I really should have dropped in a whole lot sooner."

"Haven't I been telling you that for months?"

"Uhm…Maybe…" I answer with a halfhearted smile.

"Text me when you get home."

As I mosey away from City of Hope's main entrance I spot a small engraved sign I've never noticed before:

THERE IS ALWAYS HOPE.

The 4 words split through me like a phaser set to stun.

A drifting heart-shaped red balloon.
A stenciled young girl with a stenciled outstretched arm.
There is always hope.

"You have no idea of everything you've just been through," Jen says. "Do you?"

You shake your head no.

"They had to open you up 4 times."

You can't really speak so you hold up 4 fingers to confirm that her number is accurate.

"Yes, 4 times." She nods. "There was a bypass, quadruple bypass, an LVAD and RVAD, and an aorta balloon pump that was put in when you were still at San Antonio. They will be opening you up a fifth time for the transplant. You've been through a lot. We all have."

This is the first time you've heard it all laid out like that. It doesn't seem possible. Like something that must have all happened to someone else. You don't even know what an aorta balloon pump is.

The ABP (Aorta Balloon Pump) is a mechanical device consisting of a cylindrical polyethylene balloon mounted on a flexible catheter. It decreases myocardial oxygen demand while increasing cardiac output, thereby increasing coronary blood flow and myocardial oxygen delivery. The device is inserted into the aorta through the femoral artery in the leg and guided into the descending aorta, approximately 2 cm from the left subclavian artery. The balloon actively inflates in diastole increasing blood flow to the coronary arteries, augmenting coronary perfusion. The balloon actively deflates in systole ejecting blood from the left ventricle, increasing the cardiac output by as much as 40 percent.

The balloon is inflated with helium, an inert gas with a lower molecular weight than room air that is easily absorbed into the bloodstream in case of rupture. The lighter weight of helium also produces faster inflation and deflation times than conventional room air. The pump is generally measured by the volume of gas it contains, with sizes ranging from 2.5 mL for infants to 50 mL for large adults. Balloon size generally depends on the patient's height and aortic diameter. Inflation of the balloon can be triggered according to the patient's electrocardiogram, blood pressure, pacemaker, or a pre-set internal rate.

I'm always making CD mixes for her. They are musical brews. A little Etta James here. A little Abba there. No Dylan. She hates Dylan. Maybe hate is too strong a word. She likes Dylan's words but can't stand his voice. Slip in some Radiohead. Maybe a song by Beyoncé. I don't care for Beyoncé but she does. As I finish the latest mix I wonder what to put on the cover. It's been rough on her lately. She's been worrying even more than usual. They are raising her rent again. She only has a few months before her lease runs out to find a new place. She doesn't want to move but she has to. Make the CD cover something uplifting.

What would make a perfect cover? It finally comes to me. It's an image by graffiti artist Banksy. It's a favorite of mine. I like it so much I have a framed print of it purchased a month or so ago hanging in my living room. It's a black and white image of a small girl that's been stenciled on the side of an inner city wall. The girl has one arm outstretched towards a bright red heart shaped balloon that drifts above her, just outside her reach. Directly to her left the words "THERE IS ALWAYS HOPE" have been hastily scratched in.

Yes, this is the perfect cover. I hit print.

"I was reaching for something to play as I raced to the hospital tonight and this is the CD that fell out of my glove compartment," Jen says to Loretta. "I just had to share this with you. It's eerie. Like he needed you to see this too."

Jen hands Loretta the Banksy covered CD. Loretta's hand shakes as she glances down at the CD cover and back up at Jen in the San Antonio Hospital waiting room. She starts breaking down. "Thank you Jen. Thank you so much," she says as she gives Jen a tearful embrace. "'THERE IS ALWAYS HOPE'. This is exactly what I need to hear right now."

```
Caring Bridge
July 9 2012 12:33pm -- posted by dennis
```
We celebrated Harmonie's birthday on Loretta's patio yesterday. Nice shaded area where we were able to eat and joke around for a few hours. Continues to be overwhelming to look at the faces at these gatherings knowing that just a few months ago these were the same faces filled with sadness and sorrow in gray 4am waiting rooms.

Today marked 6 months since I collapsed.

4 months since I've been home.

And 2 months since I've been able to sit inside a room that wasn't my apartment or a hospital.

This is the way I measure time now.

I do this not to gauge how bad it was but how far it is I've come.

```
From: Dennis
To: Jen
Subject: April Anniversary
```
Jennifer,
It was a year ago today. I am dropping you a line to tell you how grateful & thankful I am to you for all of the incredible, sweet & near impossible acts of love that you performed when my brother was sick. All of us had a huge role in his being alive today, but were it not for you and your tenacity on the first day he fell ill, I

don't know that he would be alive today. I also know that without your loyalty, compassion & take charge action over those long months after he fell ill, that even with a recovery, it would not have been as quick a flight. You are an incredible person, one of action, not talk. Sending you all of my love and the deepest of gratitude. Apologies for this being an email, I still reside firmly in the 20th century and wanted to send a card but don't have your new address, so pretend like the cover of this would-be card is Wonder Woman flying Allen in her invisible jet over to Urgent Care.
Love you,
    Dennis

    It is 5 am. I am in the backseat of Loretta's car with a pillow buckled soundly across my chest. We are on the 10 Freeway, just about to hit Pasadena, on the way to my monthly clinical appointment at Cedars when she turns down Journey's "Faithfully" and turns her head my way. "I'd get so torn. Wanting to be there for you. Wanting to be there for Harmonie. Needing to be there at work. I don't know, I really don't know, how I kept myself together," she says with a sigh of relief. "Every day was a foggy stitched-together haze. Drop Harmonie off at school. Go to work and hope my clients at the salon wouldn't be able to tell I was more focused on my phone, desperately waiting for a positive update, than on them. Pick Harmonie up from school. Drop Harmonie off with Catherine or a member of my prayer group. Maybe eat, maybe not. Head to Cedars. . .

    "Remember how afraid I used to be of taking the freeway into L.A.? Not anymore... not anymore..."

# THERE IS A LIGHT THAT NEVER GOES OUT

IVs dripping down like vines.

Chirping equipment.

An adjustable bed.

And a solitary chair.

Welcome to the "miracle room."

That's how your room at Cedars-Sinai is sometimes referred to - "the miracle room." The "miracle room" is the room where Michelle Johnson had been. Johnson, a 39-year-old mother of three, was successfully implanted with the world's first wearable power supply for an artificial heart back in January.

There are no windows in the "miracle room" but there is light.

"This is going to feel tight," the nurse says. "But that's alright it needs to be tight."

"That's fine...I think I'm starting to get used to it." you softly murmur.

You are getting used to it. In those moments in between the old gauze coming off and the fresh gauze going on it feels as if the gauze is still there. It's as if the gauze were a phantom limb.

Before they apply the fresh gauze your chest must be wiped clean. The gel is cold. It is always cold. The warm voice of your singing nurse makes it feel a little less cold.

*'Cause you, you light up my life*

She tosses the old gauze to the small tray at her side. The old gauze is a flowering meadow of dried brown bloody splotches. She continues singing.

*You give me hope to carry on*

She grabs an antiseptic wipe and pushes it firmly across your freshly shaven, stapled, stitched chest not missing a note.

*You light up my days*

She grabs another antiseptic wipe and repeats the same pattern.

*And fill my nights with song*

The fresh gauze gets wrapped tightly around your chest.

*It cant be wrong, when it feels so righhhht*

The chorus kicks in.

*You liiiight up myyyyyy life*

You close your eyes as the gauze and the lullaby finish wrapping and unwrapping themselves around you.

The number 27 is a lunar symbol indicating light in darkness. 27 is also the number of IVs Loretta counted that you're hooked up to. I never bothered to count them. I only wanted to know when one more was peeled away. I didn't count my time by sunrises or sunsets. I counted time by the number of IVs being removed. I measured time like a butterfly waiting to burst from a cocoon.

I get called a miracle a lot these days. I attend church regularly (every Christmas and Easter) but I've never been the kind to bandy about the word "miracle." I feel the word has been cheapened. It's a word most frequently used to describe last second come from behind touchdown passes by the Green Bay Packers on Sportscenter.

But still, I don't argue when I get referred to as a miracle.

But what does being a miracle mean? I still take out the trash. Do the laundry. Forget to make the bed most mornings. Laugh out loud at old episodes of *Beavis and Butthead*. That can't be what being a miracle means. What kind of miracle is it that would find old episodes of *Beavis and Butthead* amusing?

Every time I think I'm done writing, that I've reached the end of my tale, I remember something else. Dennis coming to visit at San Antonio Hospital carrying a Charlie Chaplin biography under his arm and one of the staff at San Antonio seeing the word "Chaplin" in gold embossed letters on the book's spine and thinking Dennis was a priest and telling him to "go right in, Father"…that evening in early July when it was Amy's shift to watch over me and she got herself sick trying to finish off a leftover bottle of wine so I wouldn't be tempted…the look of utter revulsion and distaste that crossed Loretta's face the afternoon she dropped in on Marc and me during the intestine pulling scene of *Shaun of the Dead*…

… I'm not sure where to stop so I just keep going…

Seeing Adam enter your room at Cedars is the equivalent of catching Bigfoot behind the wheel of an ice cream truck in Alaska.

If you know anything about Adam it's this–he has a 10 mile radius that he militantly refuses to go outside of. He doesn't do freeways.

"Who need freeways?" he'll say with a shrug. "I have everything I would ever need right where I am," (with everything he would ever need consisting of a big screen TV and several shelves worth of "Rated M for Mature" Zombie massacre video games).

He is the perfect tech person for the library.

Adam is in his 30s but take away the first-person shooter zombie massacre games and he may as well be in his 70s. Adam and you are the geeky masterminds behind the library's annual Star Wars Day event. If the city paid overtime for all the 2 am phone conversations the two of you had every year leading up to Star Wars Day, the city would be bankrupt.

Adam is a little pale as he enters the hospital room. He doesn't do hospitals. Ironically it had been Adam who had researched all the cardio hospitals in the area when you were back at San Antonio. It was Adam who told Loretta that Cedars-Sinai was where you needed to be. Loretta had to restrain herself from unplugging you right then and there and driving you straight to Cedars herself.

They told Adam you were doing better.

He looks over at you lying in the bed pale, thin, and almost motionless.

They told him you were doing better.

This does not look to him like doing better.

"I…uhm…saw Bob and Karol as I was coming up to see you. I handed them a flyer for Star Wars Day. I don't think they recognized me at first. They probably thought I was some kind of crazed panhandler approaching them for money when I handed them the flyer …"

You laugh through your eyes at Adam's anecdote.

"So …" Adam says, "you have any idea of how many hours of reference desk time you're going to owe me when you get back for all the hours I've been covering for you?"

You'd like to sarcastically respond but you can't. You're still too weak to speak. You can't write it down either. Your fingers won't stop trembling.

Your communication has been reduced to a combination of facial expressions, head nods, sloppily circling the letters of the alphabet Karol had written out for you on some scrap paper, and some horrendously bad pantomime.

You respond to Adam by flipping him off with a grin.

He grins right back.

You see their worried eyes. And you wish you could do more to communicate than just nod and make obscene hand gestures. Create some comfort. But the words and the comfort they might bring won't come out.

There is only silence.

And wondering.

They are wondering if you are going to be all right.

You are wondering if they are going to be all right.

"I remember when I was told you might never be yourself again," says Karol, her voice breaking into a million pieces. "I remember just crying and crying when I heard that and telling myself over and over and over 'I don't care …I don't care…I don't care…even if he can barely speak…or barely understand a word I say…he will still always be Allen…my dear friend Allen.'"

You are now conscious enough to touch the side of your neck and feel the long silicone tube that has been plugged into it. They call it the central line. The central line goes from a small incision on the right side of your neck to a large vein in your chest allowing IV fluids to be administered over an extended period of time.

"This must be what a toaster feels like," you think to yourself as your fingers gingerly make their way around your neck and the protruding plastic IV line as if reading a book written in Braille.

*What is this?*

*How long will this be in here?*

*How long will I be in here?*

*How long till the cosmic hand of fate kindly unwraps its fingers from the pause button of my existence?*

# REFLECTIONS

You push the button to adjust the hospital bed so you can get a better view. The bed lets out a mechanical groan. It takes both hands to lift the small plastic mirror to your face. You have not seen your reflection since picking yourself up off the bathroom floor back in April. It is now early May. You gaze at the reflection. It gazes back.

It is three shades paler than Casper the Ghost's Albino cousin.

The face is gaunt and thin.

The gray thin hair has returned to its brown, curly origins.

The nails have grown like wild weeds.

The beard is Rip Van Winkle.

There are no great telling thoughts as you gaze at the reflection.

No transformative revelations.

No profound life-affirming insights to be lovingly cross-stitched for the holidays by a 74-year-old woman living in San Dimas.

There is only this:

*What happened...what the hell happened?*

*"Your heart … it stopped beating at one point … you were dead."*

BUHRTTTTZZZZ!

BUHRTTTTZZZZ!

BUHRTTTTZZZZ!

**BUHRTTTTZZZZ!**

It's hard to lie there day after day flipping past CNN, old Sandra Bullock movies, and *Sanford & Son* reruns. The TV stays on a lot. The canned laugh tracks help drown out the noise of the occasional respirator/ventilator alarm coming from a nearby room.

BUHRTTTTZZZZ!

BUHRTTTTZZZZ!

BUHRTTTTZZZZ!

BUHRTTTTZZZZ!

The VAD I'm connected to tirelessly pumps and circulates the blood from one end of my being to another. The machine pumps the blood the way my heart, like a retired quarterback, remembered once doing but no longer could. There is an endless cycle of kindly nurses wishing me a good morning and telling me which way to lean as they gently lift me out of the bed and carefully guide me to the small chair with the metal rounded arms.

"We need you to sit up straight in the chair for at least a couple hours. It's good for your circulation. Here, let's put some extra pillows behind your back so you're comfortable. And here's your remote… let me untangle the cord of the nurse call button for you. Ok, there, there. Here's the remote and your nurse call button. You just buzz us if you need anything else, honey."

"I'll try not to bother you so much."

"Buzz if you need anything."

"Thanks so much again."

The weeks (W-E-E-K-S) since the VAD (Ventricular Assist Device) was installed have been spent primarily flat on my back in bed or in a small chair with metal rounded arms pointed towards a 24-inch TV screen. This has become my routine as I wait for the new heart to arrive. An episode of *Sanford & Son* plays from above me. Fred Sanford clutches his chest dramatically and bellows towards the heavens, "Oh, this is the biggest one I ever had. You hear that Elizabeth? I'm coming to join you, honey."

TOO CLOSE TO HOME

TOO SOON

DON'T LAUGH.

A faint laugh escapes.

"Ok, deep breath…breathe in deep for me one more time… good, good…"

Another early am chest x-ray. It's 4 am. Or maybe 3:45 am. It's the first week of May. I think. Who knows? Not me. Every night around this time they wheel in the Kermit the Frog-colored x-ray machine, have me clutch a lead plate across my chest, and take some radiated snapshots. I'm used to it. Like breakfast, lunch, and dinner it's become a natural part of the day.

You got to get something down. Anything. It's been two days since they took the tube out. Get something down and keep it down. You know that's what you got to do. But nothing seems appealing except for the ice chips. The throat is still too tender. The stomach a nauseous stretch of desert. A few bites of orange Jell-o. It comes splurting back up. You pop a few more ice chips. Maybe breakfast. Breakfast has got to go down better than this you think. But you'd rather not even think about breakfast.

The sounds at Norms Restaurant play out like a favorite song I haven't heard in forever. The traintrack clattering of a table being bussed, the drifting laughter, a child wailing like a siren coming from a corner booth sharply contrasting with the silence of an old gray man reading the sports page to himself at the counter.

"Isn't this great? We're sitting here in this booth right now grabbing breakfast and you're right there. Right there," says Pat. "I gotta tell ya pal, the last few times I was in this place were downers. They weren't sure you were going to make it. It was like being at a wake with non-stop coffee refills. Order whatever you want. This one's on me. Just keep in mind what a cheap bastard I've always been."

According to the National Foundation of Transplants the average cost of a heart transplant is 1 million dollars.

… I needed some help being lifted out of the hospital bed. But this time I was able to walk the 27 steps to the bathroom on my own. I am starting to get used to my new thin and wooly reflection.

But I am still wrestling with some of the thoughts that lie behind that reflection:

*Someone had to pass for you to live on.*

*Don't go there.*

*Survivor's guilt.*

Keep going.
*Eternal gratitude.*
Better.
*Live.*
*And live well.*
*You are living for two now.*
Best.

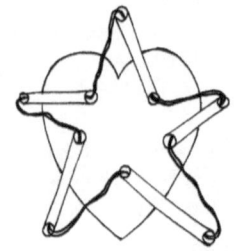

## LET US TAKE OURSELVES ALONG

"Loretta just texted," stepsister Chris says. "She's going to head over here to Cedars soon as she gets off work. She wants to know if there is anything you need her to bring?"

"No, nothing."

"Nothing?"

"…well she could bring over my battered vinyl copy of *Captain Fantastic* if she wants and we can try breaking into Elton John's hospital room and see if he'd be willing to sign it. I hear he's a few floors up."

"You are too funny," Chris says. "I'm going to text her back right now and tell her you said that."

*The curtain is lifted. Elton and his piano come slowly rolling out to the tune of "Your Song." Elton is dressed in a rhinestone covered Dodgers uniform. The piano is covered in Dodger blue shag carpeting. You are there with your father, brother, and sister. Your 4th grade self has never been to a concert before. You ask your dad about the strange smell coming from the strange cigarettes everyone seems to be smoking. You've never*

*smelt anything like it.*

Elton John is your favorite artist in the world right now. Why wouldn't he be? He plays piano like your father. He HAS to wear glasses just like you do. And he's the biggest pop star in the known universe.

Elton's voice floats above the Dodger Stadium diamond. *"...we shall survive let us take ourselves along...buh-buh-Bennie and the Jets..."*

It feels like the greatest day of your 10-year-old life.

"Till now I'd only ever been in an emergency waiting room as a concerned, worried visitor." I type from the plush confines of my 300 dollar sofa. It is almost 4 am. The writing has slowly become my therapeutic late night ritual in the months since being released from Cedars. There are far worse things that a middle-aged English major high on prednisone could be doing at this hour.

"Till now I'd only ever been in an emergency waiting room as a concerned, worried visitor."

Emergency waiting room. Concerned, worried visitor. I tilt my head towards the ceiling away from the computer screen trying to wander my way out of the maze of what to type next. The words drift, wander, and mercilessly echo. *Emergency waiting room. Concerned worried visitor. Emergency waiting room. Concerned worried visitor. Emergency waiting room. Concerned worried visitor.*

The 80s are over. Another era gone. The torn, creased cover of Rolling Stone you carry proclaims Springsteen the voice of the recently concluded decade. And there is Bruce rising from the battered Rolling Stone cover. Jeans. T-shirt. One armed raised above his head. A Fender Stratocaster hanging in front of him. An American flag flying behind him.

You are planted down inside the cramped waiting room at Kaiser on Sunset. This has been your home these last few weeks...or maybe it's been months...it feels like years. Your father and the staph infection he is fighting lie just around the corner. You are as torn and creased as the copy of Rolling Stone you hold in your hand.

*Put your mind elsewhere…anywhere…maybe try making it through that "Rise of Robopop" article one more time…*

Loretta enters the waiting room. You look at her. And you know.

"He's gone," she says. The word "gone" barely makes it out of her throat.

And then you just hold each other for the longest, quietest while.

You break the fragile silence. "Which one of us should tell the Chimney?"

"The Chimney," Loretta half smiles through her sniffles. "I forgot all about the Chimney."

"The Chimney" was Grandma Callaci's derogatory nickname for my dad's latest wife. Grandma Callaci had a way with nicknames. She was a natural. A couple of the nicknames she'd bestowed on me over the years were "the wolf-man" or "the rabbi" depending on how long my beard happened to be that particular day. The Chimney's chain-smoking habit was the inspiration for her Grandma Callaci-given title.

"I'll call the Chimney," Loretta says. "I'll tell her."

One hand wipes your eyes while the other clings to Bruce Springsteen's rolled-up crumpled face.

More silence…

*I turn my gaze away from the ceiling and back towards the soft glowing screen. My mind and hands make their way back to the keyboard. I resume typing:*

*… Till now I'd only ever been in an emergency waiting room as a concerned, worried visitor. They are sad uncomfortable places whether you are the one doing the worrying or the one who is being worried over…*

I was 25 when my dad died. I can't hear "Bennie and the Jets" without him crossing my mind. On my walk today, as I looked out across the bridge, I noticed the *Dark Shadows* billboard had been replaced with one for the new Adam Sandler comedy *That's My Boy*. That made my father cross my mind as well.

We shall survive, let us take ourselves along.

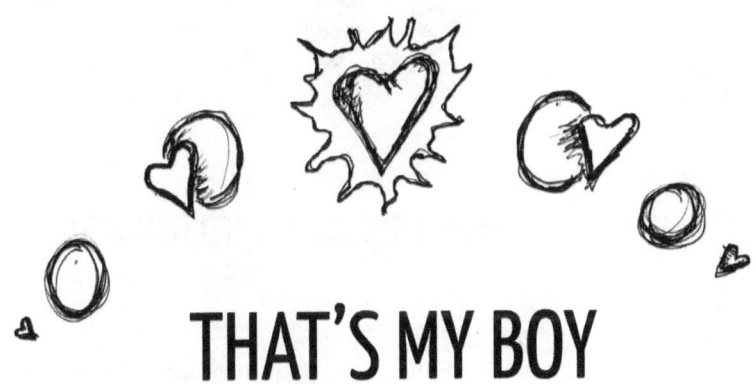

# THAT'S MY BOY

# FABLES OF THE RECONSTRUCTION

There is an old parable about a small poor man named Adelanto from an even smaller poorer village who wins a horse. He is considered lucky by friends, families, and jealous foes. "If only I were as lucky as Adelanto," they'd mutterer to one another as he'd pass them on the street. "If only it'd been me who'd won that horse instead."

Shortly after winning the horse Adelanto went out riding. The horse violently bucked him off its back like a sneeze going into a tissue. He fractured his skull. Broke both legs. And was laid up in a hospital for weeks. The whole village buzzed with the news of his near fatal tumble. Even his most jealous foes now considered him unlucky for having won the horse. "Poor unfortunate, unlucky Adelanto," they'd mutter to one another as he'd wheel his way past them on the street. "I'm so fortunate and so grateful not to have won that horse."

A war breaks out. Adelanto is not recruited due to the injuries he sustained from being thrown from the horse. Many of those who did get recruited do not make it back. Those that do make it back are never the same.

As his wife passes him some salt and the laughter of his two children seated on the other side of the supper table fills his ears, Adelanto thinks how lucky, blessed, and fortunate he is for having won the horse and how even more lucky, blessed, and fortunate he has been for having been thrown from it.

It is only through the prism and distance of time that the good and the bad can truly be distinguished and recognized. They cannot be accurately calculated in the present; they can only be experienced.

There are four and a half shopping days left until Christmas. Ten more days left in the year. And two more days left till the end of the world if the old Mayan calendar is to be believed. Isabel and I are having lunch at the same Italian restaurant we ate at the day I was taken to Urgent Care.

"As long as I've known you, you've always said even-numbered years are the luckier years," she says. "Do you still believe they're luckier after everything that's happened this year?'

"More than ever."

You were the second sickest patient at Cedars-Sinai cardio ward when you arrived. The one patient who'd been sicker than you never made it out.

Rael is here. He hasn't seen me in well over a month. We'd spent practically every Sunday together since he was 4 years old. Sundays filled with Slurpees, Simpsons, and In-N-Out burgers. Rael is now 17. I've seen Rael through from Batman and Pokemon to skateboards and punk rock. He has never seen me like this. He has a troubled look on his face as he enters the hospital room.

"Hey Uncle Allen," he quietly intones.

"So what do you think of my new look?" I ask, rubbing my beard. "Pretty Grizzly Adams isn't it?"

He's 17. He probably doesn't have the slightest clue as to who or what a Grizzly Adams even is.

Rael had tried to see me a few weeks earlier but it was too tough. Too much for him. How could it not be? He tried.

*I'm sorry Rael. This is rough. I know. You're 17. You should be busy thinking about saving for that first car... or about how to talk to that cute girl in braces wearing a Misfits t-shirt who sits 4 seats up from you in basic algebra...or practicing the 4 basic chords that make up every Ramones song ever written...not this ...*

There are still the tubes and IVs and low moaning machines covering me as there had been that last time he had tried to see me but there are now fewer of them. I've got some color back. I can speak. I've even started to walk.

*... You should be discovering those first 4 albums by the Replacements like I did when I was about your age...the Replacements can tell you what it's like to be your age in two lines better than anyone else ever will..."your age is the most difficult age/ everything just drags and drags"...they also do a pretty amazing cover of "Black Diamond" by KISS...be thankful you are far too young to have gone through a KISS phase and that there are no photos of your 11-year-old self in crooked Ace Frehley make-up to be embarrassed by when you finally get around to asking that cute girl in the Misfits t-shirt who sits 4 rows up from you and bring her over to meet your parents ...*

He looks relieved as he looks me over. Assured. He is dressed primarily in black. Half his head is shaved. The other half has been given over to his red orange hair which he has let grow and touch down to his shoulder.

"Actually, the beard's not that bad a look," he tells me.

"Maybe not," I say. "But it itches like you wouldn't believe. I can't say I'd recommend it."

He laughs.

A little.

But only a little.

### Discomfort Theater Presents: Post-Transplant Awkward Moment #17

"*Whoa*…Oh God, I didn't see you there…you almost gave me a heart attack!"

Long strained uncomfortable pause.

"Oh shit…I'm sorry…I meant to say you startled me."

"So, how does it feel to be given a second chance at life?"

I get that question a lot.

I never know how to answer. No answer I could give would ever feel complete. No gratitude expressed would ever seem enough. I think about my donor, their family, their loss. I think about the entire crew at Cedars who devote their entire lives making sure that people like me are still here to go on. I think about every tear-filled bedside visit, and all the love and soft landing prayers that were sent my way. The things that will linger like shadows always.

"So, how does it feel to be given a second chance at life?"

Why is it that we limit ourselves to asking only those who have passed through death about life's second chances when every morning crawled out of bed is a second chance at life for anyone willing to take hold of it?

Harmonie's handcrafted Get Well card:

*With joyful blessing*
*From the heart of gold*
*For someone special, who is true and bold.*
*I'm so happy you're my uncle.*
*I'm so happy I could pee.*
*Yipee! Yipee! Yipee!*

I never felt more helpless and vulnerable than when I'd reach over to buzz the nurse and announce I needed to urinate. There were stretches where I had to repeat my request several times because my voice was so weak and so gone. Imagine trying to have to place an order to urinate through a broken drive-thru speaker.

The nurse would bring in a plastic bottle and help me place it over myself as I laid flat across the bed. Sometimes it'd be a false alarm. The inner-Catholic guilt would kick in and I'd feel bad for having taken them away from more serious and pressing concerns. Other times not all the urine would wind up in the bottle and I'd feel even worse.

Thank God no camera crews or reporters were standing nearby.

"Hello Mr. Callaci, we're from *U.S. News & World Report*. We'd like to speak with you. You got a minute?"

"Sure. I've got more than a few minutes actually," I tell them gesturing from my bed to the monitors, IV, and the RVAD and LVAD machines. "I'll be here awhile."

*U.S. News & World Report* wants to interview me? Is this a hallucination? Maybe. I'm not that far removed from those sedated hallucinations of a few weeks back.

*...floating...a leaf atop a river...Leon Russell's "Song for You" playing out from some hidden nowhere...*

They hand over the consent forms. This is real. For while hallucinations may involve strange flashes of slow moving colors, pretzel twisted paranoid perspectives, and Leon Russell soundtracks they never involve consent forms needing to be signed.

I'm weak and shaking as I sign. My signature bears a strong resemblance to the lone squiggly hair that sits in the center of Charlie Brown's forehead.

Each year *U.S. News* publishes a special issue devoted to the best hospitals in the country. Once again Cedars-Sinai has been selected. They want their story to focus on Cedars' highly ranked transplant program. They'd like to speak with me and two other transplant patients currently residing at Cedars.

### CLICK

I wish the Grizzly Adams beard was gone already as they take a couple quick pictures.

### FLASH

"...and one more quick pic before we begin the interview..."

### CLICK

"When will this be hitting the stands?"

### FLASH

"Sometime around early August."

I fast forward and rewind my story for them from the bathroom floor to the transplant recipient list.

"...any idea about when that transplant may happen?"

"They're saying it could be as soon as next week."

"It's amazing isn't it?"

"...yeah, completely amazing," I add as the photographer tucks away her camera and the reporter closes shop. "Good luck with your story."

"No. Good luck with yours."

## WAIT WATCHERS

"We think we've found a match."

There are no words to adequately convey my joy, gratitude, and relief. I sloppily clap my hands together like a poorly trained seal to the rhythm of the words:

…theyvefounndamatch…THEYVEFOUNDAMATCH… theyvefoundamatch …

Between each out-of-sync clap I instinctively begin creating a mental list of all that I am still here to capture and hold…*Dennis and I trying to compose rock 'n' roll epics in his small music room as quietly as we can so as not to wake Henry…garlic mashed potatoes…Jen dryly answering "the sky" as I over-enthusiastically greet her for the umpteenth time with a "what's up?"…side 2 of Dylan's* Blood on the Tracks…*Loretta singing along to Fleetwood Mac's "Don't Stop" at the top-of-her-lungs with a liberating disregard …*

"As exciting as this is, keep in mind that it is not uncommon for a heart to arrive and be determined inadequate. When this happens the surgery is canceled. This can happen even hours before the scheduled surgery. If this should happen it could be a little longer."

*If I have to wait a little longer I will wait a little longer.*

*It is not uncommon to wait a year or more for a transplant. I was lucky (or unlucky) enough to be in such serious shape at such a young age that I was placed atop the transplant list. It has barely been a month.*

*The quick turnaround means I will not be sent home with a ventricular assist device (VAD) in me until a transplant can be found.*

**What is a VAD?**

The ventricular assist device, VAD, is a kind of mechanical heart. It's placed inside a person's chest, where it helps the heart pump oxygen-rich blood throughout the body.

Unlike an artificial heart, the VAD doesn't replace the heart. It just helps it do its job. This can mean the difference between life and death for a person whose heart needs a rest after open-heart surgery, whose heart is too weak to effectively pump on its own. or who is waiting for a heart transplant.

**How does a VAD work?**

Like the heart, the VAD is a pump. One end hooks up to the left ventricle -- that's the chamber of the heart that pumps blood out of the lungs and into the body. The other end hooks up to the aorta, the body's main artery. A tube passes from the device through the skin. The outside of the tube is covered with a special material to aid in healing and allow the skin to regrow.

The pump and its connections are implanted during open-heart surgery. A computer controller, a power pack, and a reserve power pack remain outside the body. Some models let a person wear these external units on a belt or harness outside.

The power pack has to be recharged at night.

### What Are the Benefits of a VAD?

A VAD restores normal blood flow to a person whose heart has been weakened by heart disease. This relieves symptoms such as being constantly tired or short of breath. And sometimes it lets the heart recover normal function by giving it a chance to rest.

She laughed more than she smoked. And she'd been smoking for more than 50 years. That was my fiery redheaded Aunt Eileen. She loved the Lakers ("MY Lakers" as she preferred to call them) as much as she hated bullshit. "Life's too short for bullshit" was a common refrain of hers. I was maybe 5-years-old when I first heard her mutter it. There are far worse things for a 5-year-old to overhear.

It was my Aunt Eileen who volunteered to be trained and meticulously go over all the information regarding the VAD when it looked like I might be sent home on the VAD for an undetermined length of time.

"Thank you so much for volunteering to be the one to do this," Loretta told her. "I'd be scared shitless. What if the battery isn't charging right? There's a defective outlet? Or a power outage? And the battery in the VAD dies…his heart stops and…"

"Loretta…Loretta…we are all going to do what we need to do…"

"I wish I could be as strong as you."

"You are."

My Aunt would share with us later how she would pull over to the side of the road and weep for spells of up to 15 minutes before entering or leaving Cedars-Sinai. She did this to maintain a strong and stoic demeanor she hoped would be contagious to the rest of us.

Grief is a baton being passed from one runner to the next in a relay race until the finish line is crossed. It is a weight that each person carries as far and as long as they can. And then hands off to another to carry while they catch their breath and regain their strength and wait their turn for the next lap where they will be approached by a weary teammate and asked to carry it once again.

*It won't be long.*

*That's what they said.*

*That's what I believe.*

*I am status 1A on the donor list…precariously balancing at the top of the charts like an egg on a spoon…a critical case being mechanically kept alive in ICU until a matching heart can be found.*

*They thought they found one yesterday.*

*Almost.*

*Not big enough.*

*It was a far better match for the woman the next room over.*

*I am going to make it through this year if it kills me.*

## THAT'S LIFE

Room #102 San Antonio Community Hospital, Upland, California. Friday April 20, 2012.

10:53pm – The heart stops beating.

10:54pm – The heart resumes beating.

*Every moment of light and dark is a miracle - Walt Whitman*

"Why can't we just let this go. Move on. Why are you always bringing this up and constantly pressing me about how I'm dealing with all of it?"

"Because Jen, every time I bring this up with you I get cut short and told to move on," I answer.

"I'm happy, ok? Happy you pulled through. Happy I was there for you. And I'd be happy to do it all again no questions asked if God forbid I had to. What more do you want from me?"

"To start being more open so you can start healing."

"I don't do touchy-feely."

"Jen, do you remember the last time we saw each other before you drove me to Urgent Care?"

"I don't know."

"It was a few weeks before *it* happened. It was you and I, in another useless spat, barely making eye contact as we made our way across the Wondercon floor with our nerd herd of friends... we were as tightly sealed off from one another as the overpriced *Space: 1999* action figures still sealed in their ORIGINAL BOXES that we tensely walked by...we left that day without a goodbye..."

"I don't need to relive that drama..."

"That could have been the last time we saw each other... the atonal, dissonant note we ended on..."

"I said I don't want to talk about it."

"Ok, ok... I just wanted to say thanks for being there, Jen. Some debts can never fully be repaid."

"It's not a debt. And you don't need to say thanks."

"No Jen, I do."

**The Top 3 regrets you're LEAST likely to have on your deathbed:**

1. I wish I wouldn't have missed last nights episode of the Kardashians.
2. If only I'd spent more time trying to get to that next level on Angry Birds.
3. If only I'd kept myself more distant and removed from those I love.

"The important thing is to keep going," Bill, a gracious Heart Family volunteer, tells me. The Heart Family volunteers at Cedars-Sinai are a support group consisting of people who've made it through transplants and bypasses and are there to offer their wisdom and guidance and share their experiences with current cardiac patients.

Bill is in his early seventies. Trim and fit. A laid back Southern Californian manner.

"Callaci…that's an Italian last name isn't it?"

"It's Sicilian."

"Then I bet you love Sinatra, don't you?"

"You don't really have a choice about whether you like Sinatra or not when you're Italian."

"You may just be right about that," Bill softly chuckles. "Here, I want you to hold onto this while you're waiting for that new heart to come in…there's lots of Sinatra on there."

Bill hands me an aqua-green iPod as he hums a few bars of Sinatra's "That's Life." *That's life…that's what all the people say…you're flying high in April…*

"I can't take your iPod, Bill," I say, interrupting his crooning. "…that's sweet…but I hardly know you…if something happened to it …"

"I'm leaving it here for you. You won't be needing it long. You're going to get that new heart and get it quick. You're such a young guy. You've got so much road ahead of you."

With that Bill places the iPod firmly on the bedside tray. He goes on about how great the body feels once the transplant happens and the body starts adapting. "It's like putting a new engine in a car. You're back out there travelling, dancing, golfing …everything… well, everything but sushi. No sushi or steaks cooked rare. You need to be careful about bacteria. You don't want to get that new heart infected."

"I've never really cared for sushi."

"Well, looks like you'll be set. Me, I really miss my sushi sometimes."

I look into his eyes and at his half broken smile and see how much he misses the sushi.

"Hey, one more thing," Bill adds as he heads towards the door. "My card is there if you want to talk in between Sinatra tunes. I'm here. Don't be afraid to call. I know firsthand how overwhelming it can be when you first hear you'll be receiving a transplant."

"A transplant…a heart transplant?"

"Yes, they're hoping it will happen sooner rather than later. I know it's a lot to take in right now, little brother."

"One minute you're at work feeling a little queasy and the next thing you know you awaken in a hospital bed heading for a heart transplant…it's uhm…it's definitely a lot to process."

*Where to begin?*

    *Where to begin?*

        *Where to begin?*


"I can only imagine," Loretta says as she clears her way through the jungle of dangling IV lines and gives me a partial hug.

I have awoken to a different world.

Not a better one.

Definitely not a worse one.

Just a different one.

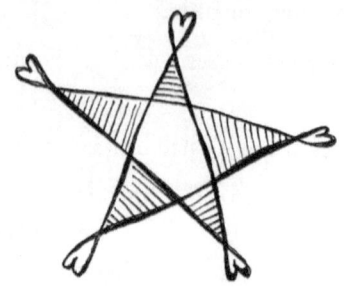

## TO BE BORN AGAIN

If you are waiting for the section where the orchestra kicks in and a grand epiphany plays itself out…stop. It won't be found here. This is a story without an arc. There are no ghosts of past, present, and future floating through an open window gently reminding each and every reader of what it is that matters most in life to be found here.

I embraced life before the transplant just as tightly as I embrace it now.

It's that simple?

Yes, it's that simple.

There was a study done once on people who won the lottery to see how winning the lottery affected their sense of happiness. It didn't. The people who were happy before they won the lottery were found to be just as happy after they'd won. And the people who were miserable before they won the lottery were found to be just as miserable after winning.

I was happy before I won the lottery at Cedars-Sinai.

I am happy now.

Caring Bridge
May 20, 2012 12:56pm -- posted by Chris W.

**A Heart for Allen**

Just got word that they have a heart for Allen. If all checks out, surgery will be at 6pm this evening. We will update as soon as we have news!

April. National Library Month. Sean, Isabel, and I sit in the office brainstorming program ideas for National Library Month. Maybe something based around a classic piece of children's literature. Maybe something based on Oz. Harmonie and Loretta would love that. Oz is their favorite.

The Oz program practically writes itself. Eric plays a mean ukulele. The Oz event could begin with Eric playing "Somewhere Over the Rainbow." Laura with her constant laugh and sunshine demeanor is the perfect Glinda the good witch. She can read a picture book as Glinda. We can incorporate a bubble machine into her entrance.

Jen can't believe this is the kind of thing I get paid to do. She refers to my workplace as "The Ivory Tower."

"This could really work. All we need now is some kind of an activity for the kids to do," notes Isabel.

"I know," I pipe in. "Instead of 'Pin the Tail on the Donkey' we can do 'Pin the Heart on the Tin Man'!"

"'Pin the Heart on the Tin Man.' That works." Isabel nods. "I like that. I really do. How do you come up with this stuff, anyway?"

"'Pin the Heart on the Tin Man'…oh yeah," chimes in Sean.

Caring Bridge
May 20, 2012 10:17pm -- posted by Christina W.

**Transplant in process**

We all got to visit with Allen for a couple of hours before they took him in. We read him all of his messages and well wishes. They just notified us that the heart is a good match and are proceeding with the transplant. He was in great spirits and we and the staff were cheering him on. The surgery will be about 8 hours. We'll update when we have news. Thanks for the love and prayers!!! Chris W.

The crossmatch that insures the donor heart will be a sound match has checked out.

The surgical consent forms have all been signed off on with my weak, scratchy scrawl.

The donor heart, packed in a sterile, cold solution, has arrived.

Slowly, gently, and methodically I am lifted from the hospital bed to the gurney like a priceless Picasso.

As they wheel me off to the operating room I gaze off into the bright fluorescent lit ceiling shining down on me as if I were a Van Gogh hanging at the MOMA.

Loretta's voice surrounds me.

"I know you only go to church on Christmas and Easter but I want you to know I started a prayer chain for you. I hope that's ok."

I smile. I turn her direction as best I can and give a quick thumbs up.

"I love you," I hear her call out as they wheel me into the OR and the doors close behind me.

I feel as calm and at peace as a Monet painted petal floating in a fountain.

*We are going to make it. I am going to make it. We shall survive, let us take ourselves along ...*

Transplant teams usually have less than 8 hours to transplant the heart into the patient's body without causing significant damage to the organ.

The ER is bustling like it's backstage 1977 at The Fabulous Forum and Led Zeppelin is about to storm the stage.

The house lights dim.

The perfectly orchestrated production does not begin with a thunderous version of "The Song Remains the Same."

It begins with a razor to the chest.

And then the antiseptic gets applied to the freshly shaven chest.

The heart and blood pressure monitors are attached.

The intravenously administered Anesthesia begins to flow.

Fade to black.

### While You Were Out

- A Foley catheter was inserted to drain your bladder during and after the operation.
- An incision was made over your sternum, and the bone divided to allow access to all parts of the heart.
- You were connected to a heart-lung machine which circulated and oxygenated your blood during the operation.
- Your pericardium that surrounds your diseased heart was opened.
- Your heart was removed from its connections to the great arteries, leaving in place the back parts of your right and left atria.

- Your new heart was carefully fitted and sewn to the remaining portions of your atria.
- Tubes were placed in your chest to permit drainage of fluids.
- Pacing wires were brought out of your chest cavity through the skin's surface.
- The sternum was brought together with stainless steel wires and the fatty tissues and skin closed with absorbable sutures.

```
Caring Bridge
May 21, 2012 3:37am -- posted by Chris W.
```
**Still going!!!**

Nurse just called...starting to close...still going well!

"I don't vant you to be offended but I vant you to ask you something," my Hungarian friend Lazlo says.

"About the transplant?"

"Yes."

"Go ahead. Ask."

"Have you noticed any changes?"

"Of course. I'm actually feeling better energy-wise than I was before I went in. I guess that exercise and diet stuff isn't just some urban legend. It works after all. Who would have ever thought? Not me."

"That's not vat I'm talking about."

"What are you talking about?"

"Vell, I read this article once that mentioned how people who had heart transplants can take on some of the characteristics of their donor. You understand vat I'm saying?"

"You mean, like one of those old horror movies where someone gets an organ donated from a psychopathic murderer and then takes on the cold-blooded killer's personality?"

"Not exactly. But something like that."

"For God's sake. If it'd been my rectum that had been replaced would you be asking if my farts still smelled the same?"

"I'm trying to ask something serious here."

"I don't know how exactly to answer you. I crave pears a whole lot more than I did before."

"Pears? Interesting. Interesting."

Caring Bridge
May 21, 2012 5:43am -- posted by Chris W.
**Allen's New Heart is Beating!!**
Just talked to the surgeon -- surgery went well. Heart started beating on its own after 1 second! He is on very little medication to support it right now. He is being taken to his room. The next 48 hours are critical... Dr. said only 5% chance he may be taken back to OR for bleeding.

There is too much fluid. They are going to have to leave your chest open overnight. It just can't be closed. Not right now anyway.

"Is this common?" Loretta asks aloud in a frightened breath.

"It's nothing that unusual," they assure her.

Loretta reaches for her phone and sends out her latest text update:
JUST TALKED TO DR. HIS CHEST WILL NOT BE SEWN BACK UP UNTIL TOMORROW. TOO MUCH FLUID. THEY SAY THIS IS NOT UNUSUAL. KEEP PRAYING. LOVE YOU ALL.

```
From: Chris W.
Sent: Monday, May 20th, 2013
To: Allen Callaci
Subject: One year out...
```

Allen,
I remember this day last year very well. I had spent the night at Loretta's. She had gone to work. I know I took Henry to Catherine's parents, but I'm having a hard time remembering where Harmonie was – I think she went to work with Loretta. It was kind of like how they show people on TV when they find out the woman is ready to go to the hospital to have a baby...oh my gosh, what do I do, what do I pack, where do I go??? Anyway, when I got to the hospital Loretta and Dennis were with you and there was so much excitement. I remember there was an eclipse which was so cool. We went outside to see it. It was so exciting when they wheeled you out and all the surgical team was around you and we were all cheering and clapping as they whisked you past the waiting room and across the bridge. We heard and saw a helicopter land on the roof. One of the nurses told us it was the surgical team arriving with the heart. We all sat there all night. So many people keeping vigil from home, and every hour we got an update and had divided up the lists of people to update by text, email or call. Finally it was morning, and Dr. Ramzy came out to tell us everything went well. WHEW!!!
Love ya,
Chris

"The transplant was a success but we're not completely out of the woods. There could always be complications. We'll be keeping a close eye to see how his body responds to the new heart. He'll be heavily sedated for the next few days before he begins slowly coming back."

```
Caring Bridge
May 22,2012 12:42pm -- posted by Chris W.
```

**Day 2**

Sorry for the delay in giving an update. Loretta and I talked to Allen this morning and he opened his eyes and nodded to our questions. His nurse Anna says he is doing great, everything is stable. She told us to feel how warm his hands are - if you had a chance to visit and hold his hand you know how cold they had been previously. This is because his new heart is working so well! We asked if he wanted music and he nodded yes, so he has his iPod again. The team's goal for today is to wean him off of the ventilator. He is in that "sedated, yet aware" state, so he knows who we are and is responding to commands - so that is awesome!!! Will write more later!

Loretta races in. She wants to be the first one in the room with me to celebrate the successful transplant. It should be a moment of pure love and sweet transcendence. And I blow it. I'm tired and worn and just not up for a transcendent moment.

"You're a hero." She beams.

"No, I'm not a hero."

"Yes. You are. If you're not a hero after pulling yourself through all of this then what are you?"

Lucky. Blessed. Fortunate. A survivor. Not a hero. Definitely not a hero. I don't even possess the strength to raise my head up from the feathered pillow where it rests, let alone take on Lex Luthor.

"I'm a guy. Just a guy. A halfway-decent-at-times guy."

I just want to close my eyes, reopen them, and have everything get right back to where it was. Work, school, rock 'n' roll, Laker games, Batman sequels, bullshitting on the phone with Dennis about the election past midnight, the taste of Lambrusco…

Loretta doesn't care for this approach. She has always been the overprotective big sister. One time I came home shaken after a run-in with a 4th grade bully and she insisted on dropping by the school the next day and pummeling him for me. I declined her generous and tempting offer. I wisely calculated that having my 12-year-old sister come down and beat up my nemesis would not work any wonders for my schoolyard reputation.

"Would you please cut all this crap about being a 'halfway-decent-at-times-guy'? Cause, that's what it is—crap. They told Dennis and me that about 90% of people who've gone through what you've gone through suffer some sort of depression. Is that what this is?"

*No. I'm not going to be part of that 90%. I might not always be a full two liter bottle of sunshine but I'm not one of them. I'm tired. I'm sore…I wish I could walk…I wish I had some kind of appetite…I wish I had the strength to lift my head up from this feathered pillow…*

*I ache. But not like that. Never like that.*

"If I've learned anything from all those summers spent watching hour after hour of Shark Week it's that the primitive shark mind has it right . . . to keep yourself in a constant state of motion is to survive . . . to stop moving is to sink silently straight to the bottom . . ." I say turning my head as far as it will turn in my sister's direction.

Loretta smiles a smile of relief and release.

Her smile makes me smile.

Maybe it has been one of those transcendent moments after all.

"Congratulations on the successful transplant. You must have a thousand questions."

"Ten thousand of them. Mainly about my donor."

"We can only give you the very basics. Your donor was male. Age 20. We can't tell you any more than that due to confidentiality."

"I understand."

"You can send a brief note of thanks to the family if you like. If you decide to do that sign the note with your first name only. We can then pass that note along for you."

To the family of my donor,

I will never know you. You will never know me. And I owe you my life. I don't know what else to say exactly. Earlier today I had scrambled eggs and Rice Krispies for breakfast while watching MSNBC. I showered standing up. I filled up my gas tank for 4.29 a gallon. These are moments that might seem mundane to most. But they are nothing but golden to me. And they are moments that wouldn't have been at all if not for you.

We will never know one another. But I will think of you come every sunrise.

## ALL TOMORROW'S PARTIES

"Greetings people of Earth," I joke into the iPad screen. "I come to you this afternoon with a message of universal harmony and peace…"

The screen answers back with some light applause and muffled familiar laughter.

It's May 28th. I am 3 days away from being released from Cedars. Today is also Bob's birthday. I've never missed Bob's birthday "Bob-b-cue." I can measure the years by Bob's birthday "Bob-b-cues."

2012 was the year of the iPad and hospital bed.

Marc lifts the three-year-old iPad to my face.

"…Ok, let's see if this works," he says.

"Wait, wait," Loretta cries. "Let me fix his hair real quick."

Loretta works some gel into my hair.

"Ok, ok now we're ready…" she says.

The dusty-streaked iPad screen glows and transforms into the Romper Room magic mirror as all the faces pass into view:

Steve

    Lisa

        Becky

Jared

   Dave

Joanne

   Bill…

It's like watching a reality show with everyone I know in it but me. And for the first time in however many days or weeks its been that I've been lying flat on my back in this hospital bed I can feel the breeze of home. I have been successfully beamed from my Beverly Hills hospital bed to Bob and Karol's Rancho Cucamonga living room. Their son Matt is running around with Spider-Man and Doctor Octopus action figures wondering if I've seen *The Avengers* yet. I think I hear a CD mix of summer songs I made for last year's Bob-b-cue playing on in the back.

Biz Markie?…What was I thinking?

I hear Pat's voice above everyone else's. Naturally. He is still defending that poorly executed 1998 *Godzilla* remake starring Matthew Broderick.

"How can you still be defending a Godzilla movie where Godzilla doesn't even breathe fire?" I shout incredulously into the 8-inch iPad screen. "That's like making a Bond film without spies, a Jurassic Park film without dinosaurs, an intelligent Adam Sandler comedy …"

"Hey, I'm telling you it has its moments."

Karol cuts in. Tells me how strange it is not having me there. "Want to say happy birthday to Bob?" she asks.

"Of course."

"Hey Allen …"

"Hey Bob…happy birthday from Cedars-Sinai …"

"…really wishing you were here …"

"Really wishing I were too."

A long pause.

The iPad connection starts to fade. I feel myself slowly starting to get beamed away from the party and back to the hospital bed.

"Hey Al, you really need to give that Matthew Broderick *Godzilla* another shot," I hear Pat's disconnected voice chime in. "You might be surprised."

Al the barber. I've been hearing the name a lot the past week as I nag each nurse who comes in about who to see as far as ridding myself of the clumps of hair that have grown in like thick scratchy tumbleweeds across my face and neck.

I've been playing phone tag with Al the barber for a few days. The facial hair has been itching so much lately that when he finally arrives I greet him as enthusiastically as if I were Linus in a pumpkin patch and he was the Great Pumpkin.

The first thing Al the barber wants me to know is that he is 70 and that he has been doing this forever but not as much as he used to.

"You know why I like cutting hair here so much?" he asks.

"Why?"

"Because, here the customers can't run away from me," he chortles.

He turns the razor on and begins.

"We share the same name, you and I," he goes on with his boisterous laugh cutting through the sound of the electric razor and small cloudbursts of facial hair.

"I've been told our name means harmony," I say.

"I've heard it means handsome. My wife would tell you it means trouble," he heartily laughs.

He talks about his wife of 20-plus years, the salon he cuts hair at when he isn't cutting at Cedars, and wonders aloud how much longer he'll be cutting hair. The city has changed so much since he first set foot in it all those decades ago.

"So, my friend, how much longer till you're out of here?"

"They're saying next week."

"Alright then, let's get you looking good. Let's make you my masterpiece."

The feel of the air hitting my freshly shaven neck feels like being born.

"HAPPY BIRTHDAY UNCLE ALLEN!" bellows Henry's voice.

It's a Star Wars-themed party (the perfect birthday theme for a bachelor in his mid-40s). Aunts, uncles, friends, family, friends of friends, and friends of family are all gathered here at Claremont Memorial Park to help celebrate. Harmonie has her hair tightly rolled in Princess Leia buns. Henry is dressed as Anakin Skywalker. Lisa in her vintage Star Wars PJs is the lone adult to join them in their space age masquerade. "They're not retro," Lisa corrects Dennis pulling on her pajamas. "They're vintage."

'Yeah, Uncle Dennis," adds Harmonie. "They're vintage. Aren't they cool?"

A Darth Vader piñata hanging from a branch floats ominously above the birthday proceedings.

"Come here, you …" Aunt Eileen says with a warm embrace. "Happy birthday! Happy birthday to my Allen! You know, I hung your painting up last week in my kitchen and I think of you every morning as I make my breakfast…It's so, so good still having you here…I need another hug."

SMAAAAAAACK!

*He's been patiently waiting since age 12 to battle Lord Vader. The long awaited final showdown between the two of them turns out to be a lot more anticlimactic than his 1977 self imagined it would be. The*

Dark Sith Lord gets taken down with one blindfolded swing of a green plastic lightsaber. There is some applause. Along with a chorus of disappointed groans from the younglings whose chance to take on Vader themselves has been smashed along with Vader's helmet.

They should have never let him have that first swing at Vader.

Vader is broken. He is profusely bleeding hard candy out of his cracked helmet. The younglings' initial disappointment at not getting to take a swing at Vader is replaced by joy as they race to collect the sugarcoated remnants of Vader from up off the grass.

Most years at least one person would have sarcastically asked "soooooooo...feeling any older?" And I'd say something like "I listened to 'Cold Gin' by KISS earlier today while reading an old Batman annual from 1989. Maybe a little older but definitely not any more mature."

Nobody asks if I'm feeling any older this year. This year it's Happy Birthday...this one's a real special one isn't it?'"

"You don't even know," is all I can answer.

"We need to take a picture together," says Karol. "Bob, could you take one real quick?"

"Lets do it," Bob answers.

Karol puts an arm around me. I throw one around her. "Say happy, happy birthday," I chide her.

A tear starts to crawl down Karol's cheek.

"Damn...damn...I promised myself I wasn't going to cry today... Bob, can you retake the picture?"

"I think it's time for us to eat your cake and then open your presents, Uncle Allen," commands Henry. "I think that's what we need to do."

"Ok, Henry, just a second. Let me find some tissue for Karol real quick."

I aim myself at the overloaded picnic tables in search of some

Kleenex.

"When you and Jen were at San Antonio and were in his room eyeing the monitors…you both knew exactly how bad it was before any of us did, didn't you?" I overhear Loretta asking Joan.

Joan doesn't look Loretta in the eye. She doesn't answer her verbally. She just nods her head silently.

I grab a couple Kleenex and make my way slowly back past the cake, cards, and gifts and head towards Karol feeling like a ghost.

## SAVED MESSAGES

Dennis can't stand Eric Clapton. Mention Clapton to him and he'll tell you "He's a dinosaur. Fake boring blues. Has there ever been an artist more useless and overrated than fuckin' Clapton?"

He dislikes cell phones even more than Eric Clapton. If you want to know how much he despises them, try texting when you're having lunch with him. Don't be surprised if he sardonically tells you to drop the cell phone and actually try talking to human beings rather than typing to them.

Without a cell of his own, Dennis had been using mine to keep all those on my contact list updated on my progress. Early morning texts. 4 am texts. Late dinner texts. He feels like a one man CNN. The updates keep streaming: Quadruple bypass. LVADs. Transplant.

There were some breaks in the text updates. The days when things were blackest they were just too hard to send.

"Here," he says as he plops the cell phone on the small tray beside my hospital bed. "Your circle of friends is tremendous but I never want to text anyone ever again."

"Yeah I know the disdain you've always held for cell phones. Thanks for making the sacrifice."

"Just keep that thing away from me," he says, pushing the phone closer to me and further from himself. "I never want to see it again."

The phone company came by the other day to install a landline for the phone device I ordered. It is mid-July. In a few short/long days I will be back to spending nights unattended for the first time since April. The phone device I ordered described itself as being "a lightweight plastic peace of mind that can be conveniently plugged into any existing phone jack." $69.99 for some lightweight plastic peace of mind seems like a deal. My lightweight plastic peace of mind is shaped like an oversized pendant that can be wrapped around your neck or bedpost at night and automatically dials 911 with one push of the bright blue button at its center.

The commercial for the device features a panic-stricken elderly stick of a woman flat on her back, pushing the button and haplessly exclaiming "Help, I've fallen and I can't get up."

I'm in my 40s…I'm not some frail old woman…I'm ONLY in my 40s…the CDs in my collection are Black Flag and Dead Kennedys, not Barbra Streisand and Engelbert Humperdinck, motherfucker.

I reminded myself of this several hundred thousand times before finally placing the order.

It's a mid-June late afternoon. The few weeks since I've been home have flown. The new patterns of my new life are starting to take shape—the morning-noon-and-night checking of the vitals, the three balanced meals a day, and two light protein-filled snacks of nuts or granola twice a day.

There is a half-filled colorfully dotted paper Dixie cup of cashews to one side of me. Stepsister Chris is on the other. "I remember you there. In the bed. Unconscious and all hooked up. And me there beside you hoping, praying, and waiting for a sign. Something.

Anything. I took out my iPod and put it on shuffle to slice through all the solemn silence… and out comes the falsetto swagger of Barry Gibb singing 'Stayin' Alive'…Would you think of me as a complete idiot if I told you now that I took that as my sign?"

Karol has your phone. She asks if you'd like her to read back some of your text messages. There are 300 plus messages needing to be sorted through. You're too weak, foggy, and shaky to check them yourself. You've only been completely conscious a few days now.

"That'd be nice."

As she starts to read you notice a troubled look on her face that you've rarely seen before. And when you have it has never looked this troubled.

"What's wrong, Karol?"

"I don't know if I should tell you….How much do you know about everything you've gone through?"

"I think Loretta has told me pretty much everything."

"I just don't know …"

If you'd never seen Karol look so troubled in all the years you've known her it's a safe bet to say she's never seen you act as stern as you're acting now.

"Karol, this is my life. I have a right to know. Everything."

Karol hangs her head down. "You're right."

"What is it? I want to know. I need to know."

A long quiet uncomfortable hospital room pause. Karol breathes in and lets out a few deep silent breaths. And then a trembling whisper.

"Your heart…it stopped beating at one point…you were dead."

You calmly clasp your hands together, pull them up to your chin, close your eyes and nod your head back and forth real slow. A few tears drop down your cheek. You feel so numb.

*I barely remember any of this exchange with Karol. I remember only being totally overwhelmed…not knowing what to make of it all…or how to begin to process it all…or how to respond…the circuits all seemed crossed and overloaded …*

"I'm sorry," Karol says in a quivering voice. "I didn't want to be the one to have to tell you …"

"Thank you, Karol. Thank you."

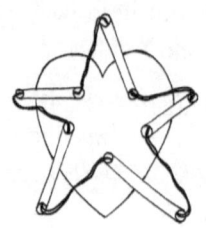

## LEARNING TO CRAWL

It takes 3 members of the Cedars team to lift me out of bed. The IVs, oxygen tank and machines I'm attached to make it a complicated dance. They roll in a wheelchair for Loretta to follow closely behind me in case my initial re-launch back into the world of the walking does not go as planned and I come crashing down. The rosary Lisa made for me swings back and forth from the portable monitor I'm connected to as they roll it around to the exact right spot. The monitor squeaks out its disapproval as they begin to slide it over.

"Ok on the count of 3," they tell me. "Turn to your left. One... Two...Three." They lift. They get me two-thirds of the way up before I start sinking back. "Ok again...One...Two...Three...ok, ok... easy...we got you."

My feet, wrapped in medical socks the color of Big Bird, touch the floor.

An adjustable belt is snapped around me that holds the battery for the VAD. The battery weighs roughly 3-4 pounds and it bulges out from my frame like George Constanza's overstuffed wallet. It will be good for a couple hours. I'm thinking that I'll be good for maybe a solid 15 minutes. "We're almost there, buddy. Almost there," one of the male nurses assures me as he finishes locking in the battery.

I remember asking Marty, a Heart Family volunteer, about the VAD. Marty told me a story about going out for dinner with his wife and forgetting to bring the charger for his VAD. That same night also brought the worst rain L.A. had seen in over 5 years. The traffic was even worse than the rain. It was going to take an hour or more to get home. He had only 20 minutes left before he needed to recharge.

"So what'd you do?" I asked him as the theme music to *Mission Impossible* ran through my mind.

"I pulled to the shoulder of the freeway and rode that shoulder all the way home."

"The cops didn't pull you over?"

"I was hoping they would. I could have used an escort."

"And you made it?"

"I wouldn't be standing right here in front of you if I hadn't." He laughed.

I tried my best to laugh along with him and not think about the times I'd absently forgotten to recharge my phone before going to bed.

The VAD battery sags slightly from my shrunken waist. I am now almost fully prepped to take my first steps in over a month. Almost. The scratchy yellow surgical mask has to come on before I go any further. The immune system is weak. No going outside this room without the mask, they sternly insist. At all. Catching even a simple cold could mean pneumonia or worse. I don't need to ask them what they mean by "or worse." The surgical mask gets quickly snapped on.

This won't be easy, they say, but it will get easier. It's going to take time for your body to adjust. It's been through so much. Make sure to keep your head up and straight. Keep your breathing slow and easy. If you need to stop at any time, then stop.

It's both annoying and embarrassing how the theme from *Rocky* will not leave my head.

My legs are like a pair of wet flimsy noodles as I stand up for the first time in a month and a half. My mind knows exactly what it's supposed to do but the body isn't getting the message. I wince. Take a breath. I grip the walker for all its worth. I need a moment.

*More wincing. Gnashing of the teeth. A little lightheaded. A little weak. More than a little weak. The distance from the bed to the door seems forever. But I am moving. I AM MOVING. A small step. It hurts. Another smaller step. It fucking hurts too. Don't go there. Block it out. All of it. Turn back to the theme from "Rocky" you got playing in your head.*

"That's it. That's it," chimes a grinning Nurse Merlinda. "Looking good, honey, looking sexy!"

"Sexy?" I grin tugging on the paper-thin gown. "It must be this form-fitting outfit I got on."

I feel like a NASCAR driver. A pit crew right there beside me. Guiding me. Ready to jump in at the first sign of trouble. Trembling hands clutch the walker. Still a little lightheaded.

Loretta snaps a quick picture. The first lap has been completed. Slowly and gracefully they guide me back to the bed. Past the low buzzing monitors. Around the permanently humming machines. Keeping the web of protruding IV lines expertly untangled the entire time. They delicately lift me back onto the bed. I feel tired. Out of breath. Sore. And triumphant.

"That was beautiful," says Nurse Merlinda in a thick Filipino accent. "I keep praying a new heart finds you soon… Tomorrow we walk twice…The day after that we'll walk three times. And the day after that we'll dance."

I longingly gaze from the enclosed bridge at Cedars-Sinai across to the giant airbrushed billboard attached like a parasite to the side of the Beverly Center. Every few weeks a different upcoming summer movie blockbuster gazes right back at me from the billboard. A sun I can see but cannot feel beats down upon the high-end boutiques, parking valets, and all the beautiful people and plastic surgeons that make all that beauty possible. I have taken to using the billboard to help gauge the time. The billboard movie ads rise and fall and rise again from the side of the eight story high Beverly Center like seasons.

A few weeks ago it was *Dark Shadows*.

Today it's the Adam Sandler comedy *That's My Boy*.

"Are you ready to head back to the room?" asks Nurse Gillian.

" I think I need a few more minutes," I answer. I am still a little shaky, out of breath, and drained from the twelve-minute walk from the hospital bed to the bridge.

"Take as much time as you need," she says as she lightly touches my shoulder. "We can wait," she says motioning to the three nurses assisting her. "We have to get you strong. We need you to be ready when that new heart arrives."

"Thank you," I say, taking a deep breath in and loudly exhaling. "Thank you." I grab the walker a little tighter and nod my head that I am ready to begin the exhaustive, twelve-minute trek back to the bed.

"You look tired. Do you need the wheelchair?"

I take another long deep breath in and shake my head "no."

"Ok, let's get you back…one step at a time…one step at a time."

I huff and puff and plod alongside her like a geriatric dragon.

One step at a time…one step at a time…

I hope the next billboard is for Pixar's *Brave*.

Please God let it be *Brave*.

High chirps emit from the wheels of the portable IV bag holders. The squawks and squeals bounce up from the tile floor as my team help lurch me ever forward back to my room like a bottle of thick, frozen syrup patiently being poured.

Walking stick gone. I'm actually going to miss it. What I'm not going to miss is the piercing lower leg strain I used to feel every time I reached the doorstep. I won't be hitting a Stairmaster anytime in the near future but the doorstep has now been officially conquered and that piercing lower leg strain the doorstep would elicit is no more.

*I used to scale that doorstep without a second thought. It didn't matter what time or where I was speeding off to or coming back from. Work, school, Autoclub, the Hollywood Bowl…it's a 6-inch doorstep… why would I give it a second thought?*

*There's a lot more second thoughts than there used to be. Feeling like I was kept around for something more but not quite sure what that something more could be. How will I know it when I see it? How do I make sure not to miss it?*

The people who've been through near death experiences that I've seen on the talk shows always talk about the glory and splendor of each sunrise or looking up at the stars and having their breath taken right out of them. I'll give them that. But for me the real glory and real splendor is found in making it past a 6-inch doorstep without wincing.

...And I remember how it'd sting every time I'd see someone 15 years older than me jog past as I waddled out of their way on my walker to let them pass. And as they'd kindly pass I'd get pissed at every double-double with cheese I ever let myself indulge in, every happy hour priced long island iced tea I ever ordered, and every processed-cheese smothered nacho I ever lifted.

"I'm sorry, this wasn't what I was expecting," says Michelle, the assistant director at the library, through some welling tears. "I thought you'd be so frail and weak and...I don't know...you look great...I can't believe you've only been home a little over a week... look at you...." She wipes a finger beneath an eye. "These are happy tears, ok?"

"I know," I say, as I take a few steps away from the walker, open the door and give her a hug. "The Force was with me."

*Most of the people who dropped in on me the first weeks I was home and joined me for my walks held the same reaction as Michelle. Like they'd seen a ghost. Understandable. They weren't able to see me while I was at Cedars...they were getting everything secondhand...and the phrase "he is doing good" can mean anything...it's all relative...dancing shirtless in a hail storm to the funky sounds of James Brown could be seen as "doing good"...being able to perform a simple, basic function such as speak in a complete sentence or breathe independently could be seen as "doing good"...*

Michelle is here to join me for my usual 7 pm walk.

Michelle is also here to deliver some paperwork regarding my prolonged absence from work. I hold off signing off on the long-term disability forms.

*Long-term disability. Long-term disability. Long-term disability. It had an awful ring as it echoed and rang from one side of my mind to the other. I don't want to be stuck planted on this sofa popping pills and injecting myself to reruns of* Sanford & Son *for another year…and another year…and possibly another…*

"Hi, Michelle," Loretta greets her. "Thank you so much for coming by and for bringing this paperwork down. I also want to tell you thank you from our entire family for bringing the paperwork by when we were all at San Antonio. It meant so much."

"I only wish there was something more I could have done."

"What you did was amazing," Loretta tells her. "We were in no state at that time to sort through that all. We're Callacis, we're not that great at organizational paperwork even when things are at their best. Thank you so, so much again for doing that."

Loretta hugs her.

"Oh God…you're going to make me cry again."

"I'm sorry," Loretta tells her as she lets go.

"They're happy tears…happy tears…" Michelle muffles as she tells me, "I'm going to wait here on the doorstep while we both get ourselves together."

Loretta gives Michelle another embrace.

"Ok, good. Give me a second to slap on some hand sanitizer and grab the walker. I'll be right out."

If there is a scent associated with my current state of existence it's the smell of citrus-scented hand sanitizer. Months later Lisa explains to me what a sad, upsetting thing the smell of citrus scented hand sanitizer is. For her it's what paralyzing memories smell like.

"You two enjoy your walk," Loretta calls out. "I'm going to call Dennis and Catherine and check in to see how Harmonie is doing."

Michelle and I set off on our 30-minute quest. A quest that goes slightly past the corner and back.

The phrase "long-term disability" does not come back up.

It'll only be a matter of days now before they'll be releasing me. That's what they're saying. I clutch the walker and waddle my way towards the bridge. The small army of Cedars staff that used to accompany me on my walks has now been reduced to one. The machines have all slowly been removed. The strength has slowly been returning. As I look out over the bridge for one of the last times I realize that the billboard outside has recently been changed over again:

*The Dark Knight Rises.*

**YES!**

Getting ready to go to the movies used to be so easy. It involved one simple step: Putting on my jacket and going. It's not that simple now. As I get ready to make my first trek inside a walk-in theater since the transplant for a midnight screening of *The Dark Knight Rises*, I check and re-check everything. Anti-bacterial wipes? Yes. Small ziplock bag of cashews? Yes. Surgical mask? Yes. Battery-powered Iron Man-looking air purifier that hangs around my neck and emits a soft blue glow? Check.

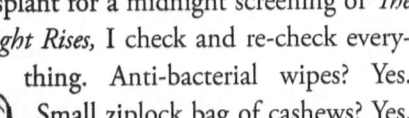

I've got it down.

"You forgot your jacket in the back of my car, didn't you?" Jen questions me with exasperation as we make our way across the parking lot to meet up with the rest of the library sci-fi club. "Go ahead. Get in line. I'll get it."

That flat tire she got on the way to pick me up isn't helping.

"I can get it," I tell her.

"Just get in line."

The Iron Man air purifier glows like a dimming headlight from my neck as I make my way towards the *Dark Knight* line.

Ok, so maybe I haven't gotten it all completely down just yet.

"Let's get you up and out of there my friend," Michael says in his thick Jamaican accent. His dreadlocks scrape his scrubs. "Time for that walk. Grab my hand. Let me help you."

I grab his hand.

"Where's the wife today?" he says.

He pulls. You push.

"The wife?"

"It's your sister, stepsister, brother, and your wife I'm always seeing camped out there in the waiting room, right?"

"…oh, that's Jen…she's not my wife."

"Well then…" Michael says with a hearty laugh, "let's get you up and walking so we can get you out there mingling with all them ladies just waiting to be mingled with."

"Tell them all to be patient. I'll be there in just a second. Just need another minute till I'm ready to sparkle and shine."

I snap on the mask. A few deep breaths. It's the third day I've been walking. They want me to walk at least twice a day. They hope the transplant will be soon. It could be as soon as a couple weeks. No promises. In the meantime they need me out there walking, building up strength, every day, every day, every day.

"Ready?"

"Lets rock 'n' roll."

"That's what I want to hear. Let's rock 'n' roll my friend."

Stepsister Chris comes in holding a coffee. "Looks like I got here in the nick of time. So glad I made it here. Seems like everyone has gotten to go on one of your walks with you except for me. You're looking so good. I swear I go without seeing you for even a couple days and everything changes. Isn't he looking good?"

"Oh yeah, absolutely," Michael says. "Now let's get out there and break some hearts my friend."

Today's walk is special. It's the view that makes it special. I have built up the stamina to walk to what is referred to as "the bridge" at Cedars-Sinai. I look out through the glass and into the great outdoors for the first time in weeks. Feel the warm sun trying to push its way through the glass. It's the closest I've come to feeling the sun on my skin since the copter whisked me away from San Antonio Hospital weeks ago. Stepsister Chris and Michael are talking and laughing. I'm not picking up on their conversation at all. I stand there silently, clutching onto the white metal safety bar in front of the large bridge window and gaze. It's like gazing out from an aquarium. The Hollywood sign beaming down in the distance, the Mercedes and BMW filled parking lot below, the crawling big blue buses Jim Morrison sang about weaving in and out of the traffic, the *Dark Shadows* billboard hanging from above.

They said walk at least 2 times a day. I decide I am going to make it 4 or 5 times instead. I am going to make it to the other side of the aquarium. And it's going to be sooner rather than later.

"Another walk? Didn't we just take one?" Nurse Merlinda jokes. "What is this, your 4th one today? You're one overachiever, aren't you? Ok, honey, let's go."

♥

I remember my mom months before the bladder cancer took her. How she resigned herself to the sofa and reruns of *Two and a Half Men*. The weight she lost. The cigarettes she still kept smoking. How helpless that felt to watch.

Don't remember that. Remember her saying how proud she was of all "you kids."

I dig down and take another step.

The cracked sidewalks. The squirrels running rampant. The house with the swinging porch chair and the "Welcome to Bedford Falls" sign posted in the front lawn in an homage to *It's A Wonderful Life*. The rusting tricycle. The one broken blinking streetlight. The realtor signs. I've lived here a year and these are just some of the things I've never noticed. The 3 walks I've been taking around the block the past week have made them all my latest acquaintances.

With the walker and aching joints the walks make me feel like I should be eligible for a senior discount at IHOP. The walks have gotten longer. I'm hoping to drop the walker and move up to the walking stick stepsister Chris picked up for me by the end of next week. I can't wait to trade in the walker and move up to the walking stick. I picture the walking stick making me look just like Gandalf from *Lord of the Rings*.

Before each walk I make sure to baste myself in sunscreen and throw on my UV ray protective hat that looks like it came straight off the set of *Lawrence of Arabia*. It's khaki colored with a long flap in the back that covers the neck. Every time I throw it on I feel ready to march straight across a desert.

Forget marching across a desert. Focus on getting past the doorstep. The doorstep is my kryptonite. Every time it enters my orbit I react to it in much the same way that Superman reacts to a shard of kryptonite: *"Great Scott! ... A doorstep!... Must...somehow...make it past...save myself...save Lois...stop Lex...must make it past doorstep to corner and back again... there's still so much to be done..."*

Today on my morning walk I walked by the house where Pat found Batboy John's body. I'd known John since college. We called him "Batboy" due to the childish scrawl of a bat tattoo on his left shoulder. He'd gotten the tattoo one drunken teenage night. John looked a lot like Sid Vicious but was a hell of a lot funnier. I remember going to a Jane's Addiction show with him in the early 90's where he threw a corn tortilla like a Frisbee towards the stage. The tortilla landed right between Perry Farrell's eyes. Ferrell stopped mid-song and admonished Batboy John from the stage for his corn tortilla tossing ways. "I might look like a clown...but last night I fucked your sister!" Farrell's onstage outburst brought out John's trademark drunken manic laughter. John loved retelling that story at parties. He'd bust out his best nasally Perry Farrell impression and burst out laughing all over again every time he'd retell it. "I might look like a clown...but last night I fucked your sister!"

I was in my 20s at that time—a few years older than John, but only a few. I knew he drank, and drank a lot, but I was in my 20s. I didn't even know what I thought I knew.

I paid John a visit at a detox center in San Dimas days before he passed. He was as frail, cold, and colorless as porcelain. He was in his 40s but to the naked eye he looked to be almost twice that age. I remember helping him lift a small paper cup of water to his mouth. He needed my help lifting the paper cup to his lips due to the violent shakes brought on by his alcohol withdrawal.

A large purple bruise, which he couldn't remember how he'd gotten, covered the upper-left quarter of his face.

Dried saliva stains marked each corner of his mouth.

Dead eyes.

I remember my stomach tightening like a fist as I left the detox center. I remember walking back to my car and desperately trying to shake the thought that this would be the last time I would ever see him alive.

It was.

His last words to me were:

"It's so good to see you, Al. Thank you so much for swinging by."

Days after that visit, Pat would find Batboy John's beaten soul and lifeless body curled up on a broken sofa next to a small plastic bucket filled with blood and vomit.

I let out a helpless stare towards his old screen door as I silently walk past.

I hear an echo.

"It's so good to see you, Al. Thank you so much for swinging by."

Rest well, my rock 'n' roll friend. I wish your choices had been different. That your path was still ongoing. And that you'd known how much you were loved and how much you'd be fucking missed. I sometimes still hear your voice. And every time I do I wish I could have done more, and done it sooner, and that you were right here, RIGHT HERE, breathing in all this raw unsalted beauty right here with me.

I remember your laughter.

"I might look like a clown…but last night I fucked your sister!"

I round another corner and head towards home.

# THERE IS ONLY THE IMMEDIATE FUTURE AND THE RECENT PAST

The gang-tagged billboards are beautiful. Every last one of them. It's L.A., Friday rush hour. The traffic crawls and sputters past the graffiti-coated underpasses. The SIG alerts seem everywhere. It's beautiful. From the smog-stained orange sky to the razor-wired freeway signs to the unwashed 1974 red Mazda with the "Don't Follow Me I'm Going Fishing" bumper sticker.

*I must look like a wide-eyed puppy here in the backseat. A pillow seatbelted across my chest. A droopy, intoxicated smile. Hanging my head anxiously out the window, basking in the foreign sights and sounds. If I had a tail I'd be wagging it furiously.*

The KLOS 5 O'Clock Funnies with Uncle Joe emits from Loretta's car stereo. It's an old George Carlin routine. "There's no present," observes Carlin. "There's only the immediate future and the recent past."

Dennis was so excited the other day when I gave him the news that I'd been cleared to be discharged from Cedars. "I remember leaving the hospital after dad passed and after mom passed. That low, horrible feeling," he said while reaching over the bed to give me a hug. "This is the exact opposite of that."

"I can't even imagine what it must be like for you right now," Loretta calls back to you. "What must you be thinking right now? You're going to be back home in less than an hour for the first time since April. I can't believe it. Can you?"

*I want to answer. I do. I just don't know how. I wish I had some kind of profound reflection to share. I don't. Not really. The feel of the June sun coming through the window touching my face feels like the touch of God. I don't say that. Perhaps I should have.*

"You're just soaking it all in back there, aren't you?" Catherine says.

I nod.

*I'll be waking up tomorrow in my own bed. In my own room. In my own life.*

There is only the immediate future and the recent past.

6 months later Loretta will confess to me that all she was really thinking on that drive back home was "please God don't let us get into an accident. Not today. Not after all the shit we've all just been through."

*There is no road to happiness. Happiness is the road.* - Bob Dylan

Making my way out of Cedars towards Loretta's waiting SUV is like visiting a strange distant place. One I've been hearing about forever but never really been. I am a shaken tourist as I float down the corridors and take the elevator down. The sights everyone had been going on and on about are now right in front of me and just as I'd imagined them. The bright lights of the Ray Charles cafeteria, the large autographed Joni Mitchell artwork Dennis had mentioned, and the waiting area which had been home to all those countless anxious moments.

Walking through the waiting area is like walking through ancient ruins.

*Everyone you love had been there. Camped and cramped inside a disheveled wasteland of unread magazines, rumpled blankets, battered pillows, half eaten snacks, Kleenex, and shaken scrambled late night calls and text messages. Days and days spent riding cresting waves of fear, promise, and prayer.*

I do my best to not break down into salt as I take one last look over my shoulder at the waiting room and continue on my way.

I text Jen: THEY ARE ABOUT TO RELEASE ME FROM CEDARS. I GUESS THEY FINALLY GOT TIRED OF MY SENSE OF HUMOR

She texts back: SO GREAT! I AM GOING TO GO POST FLYERS AT EVERY IN-N-OUT WITHIN A 50 MILE RADIUS WITH YOUR PICTURE THAT SAYS "DO NOT SERVE THIS MAN A DOUBLE-DOUBLE UNDER ANY CIRCUMSTANCES!"

I respond: LIKE THOSE SIGNS RANGER SMITH IS ALWAYS POSTING AROUND JELLYSTONE PARK ABOUT YOGI BEAR AND PICNIC BASKETS?

Her reply: LMAO…EXACTLY!

This will be the last time I wriggle my way out of that paper gown. I'm going home. Loretta and Catherine have brought me a fresh change of clothes piled in a plastic grocery bag from Target. I know what's in the bag. It seems a lifetime that I've been waiting to reach inside that recyclable bag for street clothes. I half-expect the bag to emit a warm all-encompassing glow as I open it. It doesn't. But my favorite pair of Vans slip-on tennis shoes can be found inside the bag and that's every bit as good as a warm all-encompassing glow. In fact, it's even better.

I funnel my swollen feet into the worn pair of checkered Vans with a hole in the toe. They used to fit like a second skin. The short sleeved button down shirt drapes across my new thinner frame like a lumpy blanket. The shorts are also loose. Good thing I always preferred boxers with elastic bands or they might arrest me for public indecency.

I get myself dressed and make my way to the waiting world outside. The first steps towards the waiting world outside are not bold ones. They're slow, calm and steady. I am greeted with applause, pictures, and what seems like ten thousand awaiting smiles from Loretta, Catherine and the entire Cedars staff. It's like a surprise party that's been two long months plus forever in the making.

*... I'm going home...the 300 dollar beige sofa...the dusty bookshelves...the out of order CD collection...the small stuffed Yoda*

"You're a total star!" shouts Catherine as a few more pics get taken.

*... the Vans feel tight...the shirt hangs loose...these shorts feel like they could slip down at any time ...*

Loretta heads down ahead to get her car as Catherine and two nurses help carry my two plastic bags of belongings and a slipcase full of meds. A wheelchair is brought out. I tell them I don't need it. I can walk it. They insist. "No, no you just put yourself there in the chair and enjoy the ride."

*I wonder how it's going to feel to not have to check off tomorrow's meals before going to bed...to catch a night's sleep in a bed without safety railings...God, how many weeks has it been since some unfiltered sunlight touched my skin ... I just want to feel the sun.*

Loretta's car pulls in. There's no mistaking whose car it is. BECOME A DONOR! NEW HEART TRANSPLANT PATIENT ON BOARD! has been painted across the passenger side windows in wide white capital letters. The driver's side window features a slightly smeared WE LOVE YOU. Holding court next to the smeared WE LOVE YOU is a cartoon likeness of myself that Dennis has drawn. The cartoon caricature has a comic book word bubble popping out of its mouth posing the age old question "wuz up party people?"

The exhaust fumes of the parking garage smell like a thousand fragrant roses.

*You're going home…home…home…*

"Ok, we've got your meds…your iPad…and here's a pear for you to munch on on the way back home…I know how much you've grown to love 'em…we're perfect…" Loretta calls back to you from the driver's seat.

"Let's roll people," Catherine says.

You start rolling.

*It's happening…It's really happening…we're rolling…everything is going to be alright…everything is going to be right back to where it should be…everything is going to be…*

"Damn it!" Loretta exclaims after we've paddled 35 minutes through the rush hour traffic.

"What's wrong, what's wrong?" Catherine asks.

"We left the walker at Cedars."

"We did, didn't we?"

"Shit!…I'm sorry, brother…I'm sorry…I don't know what I was thinking. Maybe we should turn back."

"We'll be ok. I'm a pretty good waddler."

"Stop going on about waddling. Your opinion doesn't count right now anyway. You're not thinking clearly. All you're focused on is whatever's going to get you back home the quickest. I can't blame you."

*It's funny. I spent my 20s and 30s treating whatever apartment I'd find myself stationed at as if it were a Motel 6. A place I'd go to sleep, shower, and shave in between work, school, rock shows, comic book conventions, and tours and excursions to Europe, New York, Chicago etc, etc, etc. I never imagined that the most exciting traveling plans I'd ever make in life would be the ones bringing me back to my own bed.*

"Let's keep moving," Catherine tells her. "My mom has a spare walker she keeps for my grandmother at her place. I'll pick it up tomorrow."

"Really?"

"Yes, really. Now let's keep moving, party people!"

… I'm coming home …

# DARK KNIGHT RISES

## WHERE THE HEART IS ...

WELCOME HOME UNCLE ALLEN! WE LOVE YOU!!! reads the large banner planted inside the small patch of lawn outside my apartment. The banner is a Henry and Harmonie creation. They have spent all afternoon making it. The banner is covered in felt marker hearts and flowers courtesy of Harmonie and some Star Wars tie-fighters courtesy of Henry.

*Look at this place! Look at it! I felt exactly how I used to feel as a kid on our annual family treks to Disneyland.* The apartment is almost exactly like I left it, only cleaner. Jen had her housecleaner come by and get it into shape. "Make sure you clean the heater vents," Jen had instructed. "His immune system is going to be frail and who knows what's been collecting in those vents in the time he's been away." The housekeeper has done a tremendous job. The heating vents have never shined so bright.

It's like visiting a makeshift set from a Clint Eastwood western. Everything seems to have been recreated using old photographs to bring back the look and feel of a bygone era. The blue light radiates from the wine fridge I picked up earlier in the year to house the wine collection I no longer have a need for. Old half-read copies of *Rolling Stone* are stacked at one end of the coffee table. Grandma Callaci's old sewing machine table rests beneath the stereo. Neil Young's *Sleeps*

*With Angels* is still nestled snugly in the CD tray.

There have been some minor changes. Clear plastic bottles of hand-sanitizer haunt each and every room. Disinfectant hand-wipes on every nightstand. A small step stool by the foot of the bed.

It is the bathroom that has been transformed most. A safety bar has been attached to the shower wall. A small plastic shower chair sits in the bathtub. The shower head is no longer there. In its place is a flexible Waterpik hand-held unit. I won't be showering—at least not standing up—for awhile.

*This looks like an 82-year-old man's bathroom. This no longer feels like Disneyland.*

Dennis, Catherine and Loretta are running around the small apartment at warp speed. They bounce and race around the place like pinballs hitting bumpers. I stay planted at the end of the sofa and watch them. I don't have the strength to do a whole lot else. Just watching them bump around makes me dizzy.

"Oh God, it's been almost 30 minutes since you took the Starlix. I'm going to get dinner started. Does chicken, broccoli, and a baked potato sound good?"

"Where should the meds go?"

"Where'd that binder we're supposed to record all the daily vitals go?"

"We didn't leave it back there, did we?"

"Wait. No, here it is."

"I'm going to put all your mail right here and you can sort through it all later."

"What else do you need right now? Anything?"

"Only that everyone just stop and catch their breath a minute. You've all been so absolutely incredible. And I'd just like to tell you all how much I…Good God, what's that smell!"

The smell of melting asphalt emanates from the kitchen.

Loretta lunges over us. "Oh shit…oh shit…oh shit…it's the potato!" she cries out from the kitchen. "I accidentally put it in for 15 minutes instead of 5!"

The windows fly open. The hills are alive with the sound of Lysol. Dennis quickly pulls me up out of the sofa and escorts me outside as if I were Elvis. The small circular kitchen table gets rolled out after us. A folding chair follows. Even from outside the potato stench can't be escaped entirely. How can one minuscule potato wreak so much havoc and create such a lingering, all encompassing stench?

"Oh God," says a hysterical Loretta. "I'm sorry. I am so sorry."

"It's ok…it's ok, " I tell her. "There'll be other days…and there'll most certainly be other potatoes."

The sun has not quite set but it's getting there.

A neighbor from across the way pokes his head out his window to catch a quick peek of his old neighbor waddling over to his kitchen table which has now been temporarily transplanted to the thin stretch of grass separating the two apartments. He quickly surveys the scene—*one small kitchen table, one paper plate filled with chicken and broccoli, the neighbor he hasn't seen in months who is now 30 pounds lighter, and the strong smell of smoke*—before discreetly poking his head back in.

Henry and Harmonie's homemade banner rustles behind me in the breeze like a pair of fluttering wings.

WELCOME HOME UNCLE ALLEN! WE LOVE YOU!!!

The greatest thing about being home is being home.

"Well, it's about time I finally get to see your place," my Aunt Eileen tells me as I pull open the screen door and let her in. I give her the quick tour, taking care to point out the high points. The IKEA bookshelves complemented nicely with the Jack Skellington bookends. The 300 dollar beige sofa. The overstuffed CD racks filled with the hundreds of CDs I've been meaning to put in order since I moved in over a year ago. The Van Gogh hanging in the bathroom.

It's like touring Hearst Castle. If Hearst Castle were a one bedroom apartment owned by a comic book loving, used bookstore shopping, music obsessive.

"Oh, I love it," says Aunt Eileen. "Just love your place. And you know what I love most? This."

She points to the framed Banksy above the stereo. The one with the girl reaching for the heart balloon.

"That is just beautiful," she says as she starts to read aloud. "THERE IS ALWAYS HOPE. Just beautiful. I can see that hanging in my place."

"In that case I'll make sure to have security frisk you on the way out so you don't walk off with it."

"You are too much," she says, laughing. "We'd better get back to your brother's. The kids are probably getting restless to start dyeing Easter eggs."

"I know I can't hug you for a few more weeks," Aunt Eileen says. "It's just so hard not to."

"I think I'll open a hugging booth in August as a fundraiser for the library."

"Sign me up for two."

"No hugs for now but let me at least walk you to your car."

A small pause for dramatic effect.

"Uh-oh," I tell her. "It looks like you got a ticket."

"Damn it."

"It looks like a large one too…look…" you tell her as you point towards the small canvas you tucked beneath her windshield.

I try to look and sound surprised. I had slipped out and snuck the canvas beneath her windshield earlier that afternoon.

I can be a sneaky bastard when I need to be.

"What in the world," she says as she liberates the canvas from the wiper.

She turns the canvas over to find an image of a small girl, a heart shaped balloon, and the words THERE IS ALWAYS HOPE. Her eyes start to well as the picture takes her in and she takes the picture in.

"Oh Allen…I don't give a shit if you can't have hugs till next month," she says. "I'm giving you one now."

## WAITIN' FOR SUPERMAN

37 every morning.

40 every evening.

Every color.

Every size.

In the proper light, arranged just right, they might resemble a piece of stained glass.

It takes a bottle and a half of water to wash down each set of them. There are so many pills packed into the plastic pill organizer it cannot fully shut.

Of all the colored capsules packed inside the clear plastic organizer the immunosuppressants are the most vital. I will be on immunosuppressants every day for the rest of my life. The suppressants act to weaken the immune system. Without the immunosuppressants the body's immune system would attack the transplanted heart as if the new heart were an invading foreign army. And it would not be much of a battle. The immune system at full strength would take down the new heart as swiftly as a wrecking ball taking down a hard plastic outhouse.

A tasteless capsule of blue and orange slithers its way down.

Followed quickly by another.

*Bottle 1: Baby aspirin-1 tablet daily-works as a blood thinner... aspirin that's an easy one...everyone knows aspirin...Bottle 8: Norvasc-blood pressure regulator-1 tablet daily (check blood pressure before taking. Hold if blood pressure is less than 100)... last 4 letters of Norvasc are "vasc" as in vascular...vascular=blood...that should be easy enough to remember...Bottle 17: Prograf-3 capsules morning-2 capsules every evening-anti-rejection med...last 4 letters of Prograf are "Graf" as is the last name of former co-worker/fellow long-suffering Dodgers fan Cara Graf...bet she'd get the biggest kick out of having her name associated with an immunosuppressant ...*

"You need to have that list of meds completely memorized in the next few days," she says. "There's no way you're doing San Diego Comic-Con if you don't have those down. I'm serious."

"Jen, I thought I was the one who was the teacher here, not you."

"Not funny."

"Don't worry, I'm working on it. I'm using schematics and visualizations."

"I don't care about your schematics and visualizations. I just need you to get it down and get it down soon. Comic-Con is only three weeks away."

"Schematics, connections, and visualizations happen to be some of the most effective tools in processing and learning information. Here's how it works. Norco, for instance, that's the medication they want me to take as needed for pain. Norco is also where I lived until I was age 5...kind of ironic that the city of my childhood would have a pain medication named after it, don't you think?"

"I could care less about Norco...All I care about is that you have that list of meds memorized by next week, ok?"

"Hey, could you slip me some Norco, I'm beginning to feel a great pain coming on right about now," I crack.

"That's not funny either," she snaps.

*"I had another nosebleed. It was a light one. The blood was not even enough to reach my upper lip. That's good, right?"*

*"Is it ok to begin showering standing up next week?"*

*"How about driving?"*

The above questions are all included on the creased paper I pull from my wallet. I have taken to making a laundry list of the fears, doubts and discomforting questions that arise in-between my weekly clinic visits to Cedars-Sinai.

When I first returned home, a little over three weeks ago, we'd been going twice a week. The two hour 5 am commute to Beverly Hills is brutal, but it can also be a thing of unexpected beauty. Harmonie fast asleep in the back with a copy of Nancy Drew, Loretta and I taking turns keeping each other awake as NPR's *Morning Edition* wafts from one end of her Toyota Highlander to the other, and the warm blanketing aroma of drive-thru coffee.

"Did you remember to add Comic-Con to the list of this week's questions?" asks Loretta.

"Nah, if there's one question I won't forget to ask this morning I'm pretty sure it's that one," I laugh.

"I'm praying they give you the greenlight, brother."

"Or better yet, the Bat-Signal."

Our laughter temporarily awakes Harmonie from her backseat Nancy Drew-induced slumber.

"I can't stop you from going to Comic-Con. All I can tell you is that it's not a good idea," says Dr. Chang. "Your immune system is just now getting up to speed. You said there'll be over 100,000 people there. It's simply not worth the risk. I hate to give you this bad news. We just don't want to see you readmitted back here after all the progress you've been making."

"I don't want that either."

"I'm sorry to disappoint you."

"No, no, no…don't be sorry. Batman never saved my life. You guys did."

"Come on now Superman," the physical therapist tells me, looking up at the framed Fortress of Solitude print that hangs above the 300 dollar living room sofa.

The 300 dollar sofa I am still too weak to lift myself off of unassisted.

"Keep your left leg outstretched just like that for 10 seconds," the physical therapist continues.

I grind down my teeth, focus past the dried, bloody wrap buckled across my chest and extend my left leg towards the heavens and begin counting back from 10.

"C'mon now. C'mon. You're almost there. How you feeling?"

The honest answer to this question would be "like a dead cockroach." The dead cockroach, for those unfamiliar, was a practice administered by sadistic Junior High School gym teachers in the late 20th century as a means of punishment for 12-year-olds who committed the heinous crime of leaving their P.E. uniform at home. This medieval practice involved having the gym clothes forgetting felon lie on their back across the asphalt playground with their arms and legs extended towards the sky for the entire 45 minute P.E. period as an example of what happens to those who seek to upset and undermine the delicate social order by forgetting their P.E. uniform. This inhumane practice was abolished sometime in 1997.

"Ok, that's good. That's good. Take a few breaths and then we're going to do the same thing with the other leg. How you feeling?"

A deep breath in. "Alright…I'm alright …"

"Ok, Superman, take it slow…a few more breaths…and lift that right leg for me whenever you're ready…let's get this done and then I'm gonna get a new wrap on you before I head out."

The right leg comes down.

The old dried blood-blotched wrap gets peeled off from my chest.

A fresh one gets put in its place.

"See you next week," the physical therapist calls as he makes his way to leave. "Remember to go over all those exercises we went over today at least 3 times a day in the meantime. We're gonna have you up and off that sofa in no time, Superman."

Superman would like to thank him for all he has done as he heads to the door. But Superman is so out of breath and so winded that Superman can only calmly smile and give him a polite wave goodbye.

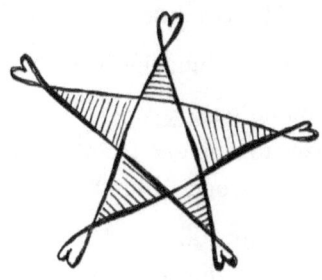

# TRUE BLOOD

"It must feel so good to be back home," Joan, Jen's City of Hope co-worker, says to me.

"You don't even know, Joan. Sleeping 6 straight hours in your own bed feels like a week's worth of rest. Nobody ever tells you how little rest there is to be had at a hospital. Can I get you anything?"

"You shouldn't be getting up to get me or anyone else anything. I'll get myself some water in a bit. You sit down."

"I have an old Etta James concert we can watch. I believe it's from 1972, maybe '73 and she's …"

I feel a few drops of moisture above my upper lip.

"Grab a tissue. Quick. You're bleeding."

I grab a tissue and clamp it down across my nostrils.

*Shit. Why am I bleeding? I haven't scraped or scratched against anything today. Why am I bleeding? And why now? I've only been home a matter of days. I thought I'd made it. I thought I'd made it …*

Joan reads the far-reaching panic in my face. "It's the aspirin. It can act as a blood-thinner. Nothing to worry about. Nothing to worry about. When you take your meds before bed tonight you need to hold back on the aspirin."

"Thanks, Joan. Thanks. I was a little freaked out."

"I know…I know. This is nothing unusual."

"Thank God. Can you do me a favor and not tell Jen about this at work tomorrow?" I say, tossing one bloody tissue into the waste basket and reaching for a clean one. "You know how she can get …"

Joan doesn't answer directly. I know what that means. I need to text Jen about everything before she runs into Joan at work tomorrow.

It takes 3 more tissues before the blood lets up.

**Blood Fact:** An organ transplant can use 40 units of blood, 30 units of platelets, 20 bags of cryoprecipitate, and 25 units of fresh frozen plasma.

The end credits to *True Blood* go scrolling by. Karol looks at me and starts crying. "Sometimes when we're sitting here like this just doing nothing it feels like none of this ever happened. Other times like now I look over at you and out of nowhere it all comes rushing back. All of it."

"I know," I say, throwing an arm around her. "I know. I get that way too."

I reach over to the end table and grab some Kleenex in an effort to help get us both through the helpless, vulnerable moment.

*Don't cry Karol…don't cry…remember that time I taunted you by sticking my stinky socked foot near your face and asking you to kindly introduce yourself to Mr. Foot… and how you scrunched up your nose and warned me that if I didn't stop and stuck that stinky-ass sock of mine anywhere near you again, God help you, you were going to chuck that half-full water bottle you were holding straight at my head…how could I resist not sticking that stinky sock covered foot of mine right back towards you after that invitation? I couldn't...and of course you chucked that water bottle straight at my head as promised...that was hilarious, wasn't it?...don't cry, Karol...don't cry...*

"Hey, I know," you say, "let me show you this piggy bank Lisa brought by a few days ago. It's the damnedest thing. You're going to love it."

"I brought you a sweet little something," Lisa says.

"Lisa, you've got to stop doing things like this. Really."

"Just shut your pie-hole and open it."

"Thank you so very much," I say as I reach my hands down into the gift bag. "Thanks."

"Stop saying 'thank you' so much. I'm doing this because I love you. The best thank you that you can give me is your still being here. I don't need to hear any more thank yous coming out of your mouth."

"...but what else can I really say to anyone right now except 'thank you'?"

"I don't care what else you say as long as you stop telling me thank you 200 times every single time I drop by."

I dig my hand further into the gift bag.

"...ok then...what would you rather I say?...I could always say 'fuck you' instead of 'thank you'...would that be better?" I sarcastically ask her.

"Sure. You know, I'd actually prefer that," Lisa loudly chuckles.

And then I pull the neon pink monstrosity fully out of the gift bag.

It's a piggy bank the size of a large baked potato that Lisa has hand decorated. Besides being a brighter shade of pink than the friggin'

Pink Panther, the pig has long flowing locks made from gold crinkled ribbon, sparkling bright purple Elton John sunglasses atop its snout, a lavender electric guitar hanging from its neck, and a tramp stamp on its backside that says "Rockstar."

A moment of stunned shock hits my face when I first come eye to eye with this beast. And then laughter. And lots of it.

"You know I'm straight, right, Lisa?" I can barely even get that much out I am laughing so hard.

"I don't know I thought you might like it," she says.

"Yeah, this pig—which is suffering from some major, major sexual identity issues—completely matches everything else in here perfectly, doesn't it?" I keep cracking. "The Tommy Lasorda autographed baseball, the Charles Bukowski books, even the small stuffed Yoda …"

I am on such a roll.

Despite the lack of laughter coming from her end I keep busting myself up and making my cracks. I don't notice the relative silence she is meeting my gutbusting responses with. Some overly analytical English major I turned out to be.

"All the women at work like the crafts I bring them," she says defensively.

*Oh shit. Now I've done it. She's hurt. Good job.*

"I'm sure they do, Lisa," I tell her softening my tone considerably. "It really is a nice enough pig. I'm just saying it's not my particular style. I probably shouldn't have

HEART LIKE A STARFISH

joked like I did. I'm sorry. What do I know about crafts and style? … look around my place and you'd think the only colors known to man were brown, beige, black, white and off white…right?…so, thank you Lisa…this was thoughtful."

It takes her a second.

"I thought I just told you to stop telling me thank you? Didn't I?" she quips.

"Sorry… fuck you… fuck you very much for this sweet and wonderful gift."

# HOME MOVIES

The sun sets itself behind the Mission Drive-In screen. The cries of a train, barreling onward, echo from behind the screen. The car radio tuned into the AM station providing the sound for tonight's feature gets bumped up a few notches to drown out the train. I grab a small handful of lightly salted, lightly buttered popcorn from the small ziplock baggie that Dennis and Catherine popped up especially for me. The sound of the train loudly hurtling forward can still be heard as Ridley Scott's *Prometheus* and my old and new life begin to play out, roll on, and unfold.

*In the backseat of my mom's old station wagon wrapped in my grandmother's handcrafted quilt. The quilt is a tightly stitched canvas of red, white and blue sailboats.* "There's 4 of us. Myself and my 3 kids. It's 5 dollars per carload, right?" *my mom asks the bored teen in the booth.*

"5 dollars even."

"Well…that's about all I have left on me," *she jokes (she's not really joking).*

*The bored teen in the booth takes the 5 dollar bill from her hand without looking her in the eye. The station wagon lumbers forward towards the screen in the dying dusk like an old, moaning mammoth attached to a smoky exhaust pipe. The effervescent scent of warm, overly salted popcorn popped at home consumes the slowly lurching vehicle. Some stray Milk Duds from the box purchased earlier at the local 7-11 so we wouldn't have to pay the drive-in concession stand prices slip beneath the passenger seat.*

*The driver's side station wagon window lets out a squeal as it gets rolled down so the clunky drive-in speaker the size of a small human head can be accommodated.*

*Movies.*

*Moonlight.*

*Milk Duds.*

"Let's only ever go to drive-in movies from now on forever Mom," I declare from the backseat.

It's been well over two years since I've last been to the drive-in.

The screen has never looked so vast.

The grainy projected images so illuminating.

The blinding headlights of late arriving vehicles so warm.

"It's like you're in some horrible movie. It's a nightmare Al…just a nightmare," Pat tells you. Tears in his eyes. Tears in his voice. The boisterous life and laughter usually found in his voice is dimmed. His older brother has just passed away unexpectedly. "I rode in the ambulance with Tom. He wasn't breathing…they were desperately trying to revive him…I knew…I-I-I knew it wasn't good…but I was hoping he'd pull through…praying for one more miracle like the one we got with you…but it didn't…it wasn't…it's just…it's just a nightmare…a nightmare…"

**Top 3 phrases I'd prefer to never hear again (in no particular order):**

1. "I shouldn't complain. I know what I'm complaining about is nothing compared to what you've been through…"
2. "I shouldn't complain. I know what I'm complaining about is nothing compared to what you've been through …"
3. "I shouldn't complain. I know what I'm complaining about is nothing compared to what you've been through…"

"Ok, let's figure out how we're going to do this. Should we use a small step stool or just try to ease you slowly into the bed? What do you think?" Dennis asks.

"Let's try the step stool. See how that goes."

It doesn't go well. The 6-inch step stool may as well be Everest. It's difficult to lift either leg high enough to place atop the step stool. Particularly the left leg. The leg they had taken the artery out of for the bypass. It pierces when I lift. "…fuck…shit…fuck…." I mutter and sigh as I try and lift.

I hope Dennis doesn't hear my R rated mutterings. I just want to conquer that step stool. Ease some of the worries for the both of us.

"Maybe we should ditch the step stool," Dennis says. "You want to see if we can try and sidesaddle you into bed instead?"

"Let me give the step stool another shot."

I wave a feeble shaking leg in the direction of the step stool again. Again the leg just won't reach. Again I mutter to myself beneath my breath, "…fuck…shit…fuck…"

"Ok…ok…Let's just go ahead and sidesaddle you in."

"Alright, alright…"

The blankets have been pulled back. I back up slowly to the side of the bed. Lean back. Plant down as much as I can plant down. My legs dangle over the side. Dennis starts to gently raise them.

"If this hurts, let me know."

Both legs safely touch down atop the mattress.

"I love you."

"I love you, too."

"Goodnight."

It's so strange being in my own bed again.

To not have a remote wrapped right there beside me to quickly buzz in a nurse should I need one.

To not wake every couple hours to be weighed or x-rayed.

To hear the sound of crickets instead of medical machines.

Zwwwwwww…The leg compressor circulators are wrapped tightly around both legs like tortillas around rice and refried beans. A soft whirring hum fills the small Cedars-Sinai hospital room. Zwww-wwwwwwwwww. A constant, steady mechanical press and roll from your ankles to your knees. Zwwwwwwwwww. You've got no strength to walk. You haven't had it in weeks. You won't have it for weeks. Got to keep the circulation going. Prevent any clotting. The sound of the compressor will be your new nightly lullaby till you walk again. Zwwwwwwww.

The thing about the leg compressors was that I actually kind of liked them. What's not to like about a space age robotic leg massage? I liked to close my eyes and pretend I was in a Ridley Scott *Alien* movie.

"What are you seeing again at the drive-in tonight?" asks Loretta.

"*Prometheus.* The *Alien* prequel."

While walk-in movie theaters are still a month away I was given the green light at my clinical last week to go to a drive-in. I did not wait long to cash that chip in. I've been going stir crazy to see anything projected onto a big screen for months. I'd even settle for a Meg Ryan romantic comedy at this point.

"Who all is going?" Loretta continues.

"Dennis, Catherine…Mandisa, Dwight and the rest of the library sci fi club. Nothing to worry about."

"…but I am worried."

"I know. It's really not all that big a stretch to go from being on my sofa wrapped in a blanket watching an *Alien* blu-ray to being in the passenger seat of Dennis' Highlander wrapped in a blanket watching an *Alien* movie."

"It just seems so soon."

"It will always seem too soon."

"I know…I know…and I'm trying not to worry."

"Try not. There is only do, or do not. There is no try."

"I like that…what great eastern philosopher is that from?"

"Yoda."

"Yoda? …dear God, baby brother…enjoy the drive-in tonight. Don't forget the hand sanitizer. Enjoy your movie. I love ya."

Yoda says that Yoda can cover Tuesday nights and either Friday or Saturday nights but definitely not Mondays. Yoda needs to meet up with the personal trainer on Mondays.

Jen thinks that it's just allergies but doesn't want to risk infecting me by coming for the scheduling meeting. Hence, she is attending tonight's meeting via speakerphone.

Dennis has grabbed the small plush Yoda that resides atop my comic book loaded footlocker and placed it next to the speakerphone. The plush Yoda will act as the physical embodiment of Jen for the meeting. It will have to do. I don't own a plush toy of the headstrong, tough-talking Leia from Episode IV we can use.

Besides Dennis and master Yoda, stepsister Chris, Marc, Bob, and Karol are also huddled in my small living room to discuss scheduling.

It feels like half-time in a locker room. With all the binders, charts, and diagrams being gone over one last time before the whistle blows and it's time to get back out on the field.

"I think it's important for whomever is there to have a checklist of what they need to…"

The rest of Jen's sentence gets lost in a rising cloud of snorting laughter as Dennis puppeteers the plush Yoda's head to move in perfect sync to Jen's voice. "Mmmmm…make sure he gets proper daily units of insulin you will."

"Can somebody please explain to me why Dennis is repeating back everything I say in a bad Yoda voice?" Jen's voice cries out from the speakerphone wilderness.

Dennis picks Yoda back up. "Repeating back everything I say in a bad Yoda voice, can somebody please explain to me why Dennis is, hmm? Hmmmmmm."

I could watch this all day.

"Well Jen," I answer between bursts of laughter, "you know that stuffed Yoda on my footlocker…right now that's your avatar…"

"You are all **SO** lucky I love *Star Wars*!"

"All so lucky I love *Star Wars*, you are!" Dennis fires back.

"Uhm…perhaps we should get back to the insulin procedures," Marc gently interrupts.

I can't believe how she pressed me last night. How she told me I needed to start getting this all down by myself like I haven't even been trying. Why doesn't she try plunging a syringe into her stomach with two shaking arms and 10 trembling fingers and report back to me how easy it all is? She's a nurse. She should know this. I'll show her. I'm going to roll myself up, over and out of this bed right now. Right now.

"What the hell are you doing out of bed? What is this shit?"

"You were going on and on last night about how much I needed to start doing it all by myself now that I'm back home, Jen...so here you have it."

"This is not what I meant and you know it! You could have cracked your damn head right open rolling yourself out of bed! You understand that? You're so damn stubborn to begin with and all the meds and steroids you're on right now aren't helping with your attitude...I'm telling myself this right now to keep myself from strangling you. You better not ever, **ever** pull shit like this again...now, what'll it be for breakfast? Cheerios or Corn Flakes?"

Meds, steroids, and stubbornness my ass. I am being completely rational, completely agreeable and completely FUCKING adult.

... Well...maybe not completely adult ...

"I don't want Cheerios or Corn Flakes. I want Rice Chex...and I can get them all by myself during the next *Justice League* cartoon commercial break."

Did you ever see that old 1978 movie *The Swarm*? The one starring Michael Caine and Olivia de Havilland about 22 million African killer bees invading the U.S.? It's not all that great, in fact it's actually pretty wretched even for a killer bee flick. It's also what my living room currently resembles. Well, almost. Pretty close anyway. Three honeybees as opposed to 22 million African killer bees. One bee on the lamp. One bee clinging for dear life onto the screen door. And one bee drunkenly buzzing around Yoda.

"Where are they all coming from?" asks Loretta.

"Quick, run inside your room. Close the door. Tight. While I think of what we should do."

We count to 3 together. On the count of 3 she helps lift me from the sofa and I begin my slow advance to the bedroom.

After a few minutes I call out from behind the bedroom door over the sound of the buzzing bees, "Hey, how's it looking out there?"

"I'm thinking…I'm thinking…why does this crap only seem to happen on my watch?…I'm calling Dennis."

"You know how hard he's going to laugh over all this?"

"I know…I'm calling him anyway."

Dennis arrives at my door less than 10 minutes later. "This is so classic," he says laughing. "How many Callacis does it take to handle a couple of bees?"

"Looks like the answer to that would be 3," comes my muffled response from behind the bedroom door. "Possibly 4. The 3 of us haven't gotten a single bee out yet."

"Don't get stung…don't get stung…don't get stung…" Loretta chants like a mantra each time Dennis approaches a bee.

Operation Desert Swarm has begun.

The bee on the screen door is the first to go. Dennis cracks the screen door a bit. The bee shoots out as if shot from a cannon.

The bee trapped inside the thin lampshade is next. That one

doesn't really count. The poor guy is paralyzed and practically lifeless. There's no fight there.

"Everything alright?" I call out from the bedroom.

"So far we're 2 for 3."

"…don't get stung…don't get stung…don't get stung…"

The last bee buzzing, the one circling around Yoda, proves to be the trickiest. That's the one Dennis has to chase around for 5 minutes or so with a small martini glass. The bee finally tires and touches down on the carpet. Dennis pounces and traps the bee between the carpet and the martini glass.

"You can come out now," he calls towards my closed bedroom door.

I crack open the bedroom door and slowly and steadily make my way back to the sofa.

"See, I was right—it does take 3 Callacis," I chime.

"What do you mean 3?" cracks Dennis. "All you did the entire time was hide behind the damn bedroom door."

There's a ring of the doorbell. The ring of my doorbell is unmistakable. It sounds like a pissed-off buzzing hornet.

"I'll get it," I call over to Loretta who is busy scurrying around the kitchen.

"I brought you a visitor," Catherine says.

"How much longer till I'll be able to come inside, Uncle Allen?" Henry's voice calls from the other side of the screen door.

Henry's full head of curls is covered by R2-D2-style Mickey Mouse ears.

"Soon."

"How soon, Uncle Allen?"

"About 3 weeks."

"That sounds like a long time."

"It'll go quick. You'll see."

"I brought you an extra Clone Trooper figure I had. See?"

I prop open the screen door. Henry drops the small, battle-damaged plastic Clone Trooper into the palm of my hand.

"You like it, Uncle Allen?"

"I love it, Henry. It's way cool."

"How long will it be again till I get to come inside and visit?"

"In 3 weeks. When it's August. I'll even be able to hug you come August."

"I wish it was August already."

"Me too, Henry. Me too."

# NEVER TELL ME THE ODDS

I text Jen. WE MADE IT! WE'RE IN! I JUST GOT OUR BADGES TO STAR WARS CELEBRATION. ONLY 6 MONTHS TO GO BEFORE THE CELEBRATION BEGINS IN AUGUST! MAY THE FORCE BE WITH US!

She texts back 2.5 seconds later: THAT'S SO GREAT! SO EXCITED!

"I'm not excited. I think it's too soon and I don't think you should be going."

"You're not excited? What are you talking about? We've had our Star Wars Celebration badges for months now. Months. And you wait until we're less than three weeks away to tell me you're not excited."

*How could she not be excited? Has she not noticed how I've been pushing myself for the last month, step by wince-inducing step, to make it to Orlando...every pill...every injection...all that broccoli...how could she not be as excited as I am?*

"Will you stop being so damn stubborn? Listen to what I'm

saying. I don't think it's a good idea...I'm not excited...I've been thinking about it and worrying about it since I saw you straining to walk those stairs at the *Dark Knight Rises* two weeks ago. I know how obsessed you've been with going. I couldn't bring myself to tell you until now."

"The *Dark Knight* was over two weeks ago, Jen. This might sound ridiculous to you but I've come so far these past few weeks. I have. You wouldn't believe it. You don't. But you haven't seen me lately. We've only talked on the phone because you've been sick. And you got sick because of how little you've been sleeping and how much you've been worrying about me. I know that...I know that..."

"If you really knew how much I've been worried you wouldn't go ..."

"And if you knew how much this meant to me you'd share some of my excitement. Star Wars Celebration has been the carrot I've been dangling in front of myself all summer long as I popped each pill, took each fragile step, sacrificed San Diego Comic-Con ..."

"It's too soon."

"The transplant team at Cedars gave me the greenlight...why can't their word be good enough for you."

"Don't go there. Don't you even go there with me. I work in the medical field. I knew all about Cedars-Sinai long before you were there. And I saw firsthand the miracle they performed on you...I was there in that parking lot night after long night desperately trying to catch some sleep in my car while you were there...so don't be going there when I'm trying to explain how fucking uncomfortable I am with this trip ..."

*How could you have been so blind as to not have seen or taken into account everything she's saying...to have not fully noticed how far down the depth of all her strain and worry actually went...her look of distant troubled concern at the* Dark Knight *screening didn't register at the time...it's starting to now ...*

"I don't want you worrying so much…"

"I have to because God knows you aren't worrying enough!"

Loretta races to the room and takes the phone from me.

"Let me talk to her," Loretta says. "…Hi Jen, it's Loretta. I overheard the conversation you two were having and just wanted to say a few things…I understand where you're coming from. I do. I was scared shitless when Allen went to the drive-in a few weeks ago…but he went…and made it through…there's always going to be that fear after what we've gone through, it's never going to completely go away, but we have to let go and work our way past…it's not easy…that fear…it's always going to be there…it will always be there…" Loretta starts to silently sob. "It's like we've been through a war together and we've made it home but we're suffering from post-traumatic stress disorder."

*Post-Traumatic Stress Disorder: a reaction of helpless anxiety, fear, and recurring flashbacks brought on after witnessing or experiencing a harrowing, traumatic event.* Yes. Shit.

"…if anything were to happen to him while we were in Orlando…I feel like it'd all be on me…"

"No…Jen…no…he's an adult. A real stubborn-ass adult. We both know he would go even if it meant flying out there by himself. But we also know he's been doing everything they've been telling him to do without question. As his sister I want to assure you that as far as our family is concerned this isn't on you, Jen. It isn't. That wouldn't be fair. It's all on him."

*Let it be all on me Jen. Last thing I want is to be a rusted anchor dragging you to the bottom. I don't want you wasting this trip thinking I'm your patient. I want this trip to be about release for the both of us and all we've made it through.*

"My mom thinks it's important we go."

"It is. It's important you go and have yourself a good time while you're there. You've so earned it, Jen. I hope this helps."

"It has."

"Love you, Jen."

Loretta hands the phone back.

"Hey Jen…I'm sorry …"

"Sorry, for what?"

"I know you worry. I know you're angry."

"Angry?"

"Angry."

*How many years was I on you about your lack of sleep, lack of exercise, and all that Del Taco? How many? How many? How come you didn't listen? You never listened …you know how close you came to… how you almost nearly …*

"Angry…whatever…why do you always have to overanalyze everything that I…"

"…ok Jen…ok…I'm sorry…If they express even the slightest hesitation about the trip when I go to my clinical next week at Cedars I won't go. No argument. No nothing. I promise. I'm sorry."

A slight pause.

"Don't be sorry…and don't forget to call the airline tomorrow about getting a diabetic meal on the flight, ok? You can't be straying from your dietary restrictions. You know?"

"I know."

"Any more questions this morning before I let you go?" asks Dr. Kittleson.

"Just one more. When I'm in Orlando next week for Star Wars Celebration, I plan on going to a couple of theme parks. Am I ok to go on rollercoasters? I know they have restrictions about riding with a heart condition."

"You HAD a heart condition," Dr Kittleson smiles. "With the new heart it will be the first time in your life you've ever ridden a rollercoaster without a heart condition."

I'd never looked at it like that. I'd been a ticking time bomb for the last 4 decades that could have gone off at any time:

… it could have happened sprinting up three flights of stairs at Mt. SAC to make it on time to teach my 8 am class.

… or swinging from the rafters during a set at the Troubadour.

… or while riding Space Mountain. I play out that morbid scenario in my head. "In space no one can hear you scream. Coming up in the 6 o'clock news hour, local college professor suffers fatal heart attack while riding Space Mountain …"

Thankfully, this thought gets cuts short by the voice inside my head sounding once again like the thick Sicilian baritone of my old Uncle Joe. I can almost smell the cigar smoke coming off the voice. "What's with you and all this god damn Space Mountain nonsense? You wanna know what this all sounds like to me? Like a bunch of bullshit. That's what. So, what's it gonna be? Stay fixated on some past that never was or make the most of this future you've been gifted."

Dr Kittleson hands me the paperwork to take down to the lab. I give her a warm embrace with every last ounce of gratitude I've got in me.

"Enjoy your trip. And may the Force be with you."

"I have no doubt that it already is."

"So Adam what do you think of emailing Mary Franklin over at Lucasfilm about doing a panel at this year's Star Wars Celebration in Orlando on the library's Star Wars Day?"

"What's a Star Wars Celebration?"

"It's the big Star Wars convention sanctioned by Lucasfilm that happens every few years. Everyone's there. Mark Hamill, Carrie Fisher…even Lucas himself has been known to put in an appearance."

"What about Tim Rose?"

"Tim Rose?"

"Admiral Ackbar."

"I'm sure if they can get Lucas they can get the guy who wore the squid mask in *Return of the Jedi*."

"*Jedi* was so much better than *Empire Strikes Back*."

"You're just saying that to piss me off."

"Maybe."

"So what do you think about proposing a panel for Celebration?"

"You've had worse ideas. Like the time you had that idea to give the kids Silly String so they could pretend to be Spider-Man for Superhero Day. You know how flammable that stuff is?"

"…so I have your blessing about sending off a panel proposal?"

"You realize how far Orlando falls outside of my 10 mile radius, don't you?"

"I'm bad at geography but not that bad."

"…you think this might actually happen?"

"Who knows? All I know is that is that it's worth a shot…and that *Empire Strikes Back* kicks ass over *Return of the Jedi* every damn day of the week."

"Did you ever hear back from Lucasfilm about that Star Wars Celebration proposal?"

"Not yet."

"How long ago did you send that out?"

"December."

"It's March."

"I know."

"Probably not going to happen."

"Probably not."

"You still going?"

"Jen and I already have badges."

"Say hello to General Ackbar for me. The greatest Star Wars character ever from the greatest Star Wars film ever—*Return of the Jedi*."

From: Mary Franklin
To: Callaci, Allen
Subject: RE: Star Wars Celebration Fan Panel Proposal
Sent: Thu 8/2/2012 5:59 PM

Allen, are you still interested in doing a panel at Celebration VI?

I know it's a little late, but I do have a space for you on Sunday, August 26th if you can do it.

Mary Franklin,
Sr. Events Lead
Lucasfilm, Ltd.
**\*Forwarded to Jen: Thu 8/2/2012 6:00 PM**

From: Jen
Sent: Thu 8/1/2012 6:02 PM
To: Callaci, Allen
Subject: RE: Star Wars Celebration Fan Panel Proposal

You're like a geek celebrity now! I'm going to have to have you autograph something!

**STAR WARS CELEBRATION VI PROGRAM GUIDE (PAGE 34):**
Sunday August 26 1:30-2:30pm
**Using the Force to Reach Reluctant Readers**
Allan Callaci, Reading Enrichment Coordinator at Paul A Biane Library in Rancho Cucamonga, California, will share how educators, librarians, and parents can use the passion kids and teens have for all things Star Wars to help them learn to read. Callaci will present a host of Star Wars tools and resources including books, programming ideas, and lesson plans. Look for a possible appearance by a special Jedi Master guest.

"So are you going to mention *it*?"

*It* meaning the transplant. It's become shorthand between Jen and me. As in her saying "I remember that last CD mix you made me right before *it* happened." Or my saying "Today I drove on the freeway for the first time since *it* happened." Or "No, I don't think I'll mention *it* at the panel today. I want to keep the focus on Star Wars and reluctant readers."

"You're such an English major. I think it'd be nice for people to hear about *it* and see you up there and how well you're doing."

"Maybe."

"Maybe. Hmmmmf. You saying 'maybe' means you're not going to mention *it* at all, doesn't it?"

"It's a nice thought, Jen."

I no longer fear needles. I fear the stage. I find myself nervous and anxiously pacing backstage minutes before the panel is set to begin. I've never been afraid of getting up in front of people. I've done panels before, sung in front of complete strangers all over the world, and taught and lectured classrooms full of enthralled 19 and 20-year-olds covertly trying to read their texts without being noticed. But this is different. This is *Star Wars*.

I imagine my 12-year-old self and his Death Star-destroying

daydreams taking this all in and beaming. There he is in his crooked glasses with the scratched plastic lenses, a tattered pair of corduroys, an ill-fitting retainer and a flimsy light tan t-shirt with a faded iron-on patch of R2-D2 and C-3PO. He has seen *Star Wars* a whoping 4 times in the theater, more than any other 12-year-old he knows. His favorite scene is the one where Luke looks longingly out towards the two setting suns and ponders an unknowable greater destiny.

It still is.

Obi-Shawn races up carrying Yoda beneath an arm. "Sorry I'm just getting here. It just took forever…I gotta tell you you're looking great…ready to roll?"

"It is our destiny," I answer in a mediocre-at-best Darth Vader voice as Obi-Shawn, Yoda and I get escorted out onstage by two volunteers. As we cut our way through to the stage I'm not thinking about the Lantus-filled syringes, or the bursting-at-the-seams clear plastic pill containers divided by day, or the not-as-sore-but-still-quite-sore legs, or the scarred and tender chest …

**… I'm here…I'm here?…I'M HERE!**

No, we don't draw the hundreds of people that Carrie Fisher would have but there's about 32 filled seats. 33 if you include Jen. Not bad. The hour flies by as quickly as if it were being pulled in by a tractor beam. It begins with a mention of the thousands of people who file into the library every year for the Star Wars program that Adam and I throw. It closes with Obi-Shawn leading the audience in a sing-along of "Old George Lucas Had a Ranch" (sung to the tune of "Old MacDonald had a Farm").

And on this ranch he had a Wookiee, E-I-E-I-O

With a
"RUUUUUrhrGUGUGHRhghghghrRURURUghGHrrrrrr"
here

And a
"RUUUUUrhrGUGUGHRhghghghrRURURUghGHrrrrrr"
there …

As Obi-Shawn hits the final notes of his Wookiee-laden serenade Jen comes up to the wing of the stage and motions that we need to get moving if we're going to make our flight home.

I nod goodbye to Obi-Shawn from the wing. Jen and I hastily make our way. The sound of Wookiees still roaring in our heads.

"You did great. I don't think I've ever seen you be so serious and focused for so long without being funny or goofy."

"…You know, I think you were right earlier."

"About what?"

"I should have mentioned *it*."

"Really? I was just thinking how it was better you didn't."

"It's a traaaaaap," cries a muffled, gurgled voice from my backpack.

"What was that?"

"A talking plush Admiral Ackbar. I picked it up for Adam. You press its chest and it says Ackbar's catchphrase which is …"

"I know Ackbar's catchphrase. Would I be at a Star Wars Celebration if I didn't? I'm not like *some* people here that I could mention who haven't even caught an entire season of *Clone Wars* …"

I start laughing.

"What's so funny?" Jen suspiciously asks.

"Oh, I just never thought I'd see the day where I'd be dressed down by a flesh and blood female at a Star Wars convention for a lack of Star Wars knowledge."

"True."

She laughs in spite of herself.

I reach down into my backpack and press Ackbar's chest. I do this not because I want to hear Ackbar exclaim "it's a trap" yet again but for the exasperated huff I know it will elicit from Jen.

"You're a mess," she says with a gentle, natural laugh.

It's a laugh I can't remember having heard since *it* happened.

A few days post-Orlando a hastily scratched note will be waiting on her doorstep:

> Jen,
>
> I know this wasn't the easiest of trips for you. How scared you were. And the strength you had to find to overcome those fears. Thank you for having that courage Jen. Courage isn't found in fighting the battles you're sure of winning. It's found in fighting those battles you're not so sure you'll win and fighting on regardless.
>
> — Allen

# LONESOME SURPRISE

I wake up. There's no one there. For the first time in 5 weeks there is no one there. I enter the living room from the bedroom and there's no one there stretched across the beige 300 dollar sofa or sprawled out on the floor on an inflatable mattress. No one to be heard bustling in the kitchen making coffee. No sound of CNN or *I Love Lucy* reruns quietly filtering from the TV. There is only me.

The small quiet living room has reverted back to its original form. I say good morning to myself in the mirror. No one but myself hears it.

HOW GOES FIRST MORN ALONE BROTHER? TEXT ME WHEN YOU WAKE. LET ME KNOW YOU MADE IT THROUGH. LOVE YA LORETTA.

The warm summer morning breeze cuts through the bedroom window and slaps me across the face. A tightly rubber-banded copy of the *L.A. Times* waits patiently on the doorstep. The cornflakes taste like revitalization.

Birds sing outside for no apparent reason, or maybe they've got their reasons after all.

Playing the songs again, like walking, showering, and driving, is essential to becoming complete again. The songs open you up, close you back up and make you new again.

```
Caring Bridge
Jun 12, 2012 12:16pm -- posted by dennis
```
Spent the night over at Allen's last night & the 2 of us played Refrigerator songs for over an hour. We did songs from memory that were written 20 yrs ago as well as newer songs that we have been working on over the last year. Was so wonderful to harmonize with each other again. When we play music together & with the band, we are both in a whole other world. And we both had that same out of body float that you get when the music & melody is hitting right. We stayed up until nearly 1am talking & playing before the night owl would go to bed, with him jokingly telling me he could stay up all night if I wanted as he had nowhere to be in the AM!

### The Lady Day 3:15am Prednisone Blues

Tapping the keypad in rhythm

to a lone coyote howling at a dying moon

and the worn blue grooves of Billie Holiday

softly playing on the stereo

    I don't know if I've ever seen Chris cry. I've known him since I was in 7th grade and he was in fourth. We bonded over Mötley Crüe, *The Uncanny X-Men*, and shoplifting issues of *Circus* magazine from the local Stater Brothers. It was inevitable we'd all wind up in a band together. While most of our peers were busy scoring touchdowns, going to prom, and smoking cigarettes in the parking lot to puncture their teen suburban malaise, we punctured ours by smearing "OZZY" across our knuckles with black felt tip markers.

Tonight will be our first band practice since the transplant. We have been calling ourselves Refrigerator for over 20 years. My 17-year-old Iron Maiden-loving self would have abhorred the name Refrigerator.

I enter the rehearsal studio and make my way past the faded band flyers and handcrafted Tiki bar. "Hey, Nacho," I say pinching my fingers together in the shape of heavy metal devil horns, "you ready to rawwwwwk the clubhouse dowwwn?"

"Nacho" was the nickname bestowed upon Chris at a Redding Taco Bell during a West Coast tour in the early '90s. "The Clubhouse" was the nickname given to the small industrial space we'd been practicing at for years. Well, not practicing exactly, but where the four of us (Dennis, myself, Chris and bass player Daniel) gathered occasionally to drink beer, deride Eric Clapton, mock Daniel's whimsical Canadian accent, and just maybe go over a song or so.

*When was the last time we played together? Was it last February? No. Last October? Maybe.*

We decide to play "Lonesome Surprise." One of our oldest songs. Something warm and familiar.

>Doctor, doctor
>
>Can you help me, please?

*I wonder if we'll ever sound the way we once did. So many false starts and stops. So much collected dust to be shaken.*

>I had a name,
>
>I had a place
>
>But like the clothes I wear
>
>The holes grow everywhere
>
>til it's like having nothing at all ...

*I have no idea how we sound right now. I only know it feels electric to be connected and plugged back in. Distorted. Amplified. Feeding back. A wave of emotion crashing all around. It reminds me of something Dennis once said about music being a far more healing force than any amount of tears or sorrow sent to a vacant sky.*

        Here's your lonesome surprise,

            lonesome surprise,

            lonesome surprise

*Tears are streaming from Chris' eyes.*

I've never seen him cry.

    So it's maybe my third day at work at the Upland Library as a junior clerk. A junior clerk does everything a senior clerk does at the library only less of it. There's a call on the library line in the back room. It's John from the Mountain Goats. He's calling from a radio station in the Netherlands. It makes perfect sense. *Who else but John, asking you to sing "Lonesome Surprise" with him live on a radio station broadcast, would be calling the Upland Public Library at this odd hour of 1:37 in the afternoon?*

    John had felt bad that we hadn't been able to join him to play a festival in the Netherlands. Between Dennis and Catherine having just had Rael and my recently launched and ever-promising career as a part-time junior clerk at the Upland Public Library, we just weren't able.

    A few weeks earlier John and I had been killing time loitering in the parking lot outside a Claremont café. "I'm telling you, if there was anything I could humanly do to get that voice of yours to the people of the Netherlands I'd do it," John proclaimed. "Damn straight I'd do it."

    John was always making grand parking lot proclamations like that.

    And sometimes grand parking lot proclamations turn into grand realities…

...is this really happening?...a transcontinental duet of "Lonesome Surprise" spanning from the basement of the Upland Public Library to the Netherlands airwaves...can they fire me for this?... there was nothing in the employee manual implicitly forbidding employees to take part in international broadcasts during work hours...

Right before we are about to go live a co-worker walks in. She has a question for me. I ask her if it can wait a few minutes until I'm done dueting with a friend for a live international radio broadcast.

She nods and holds onto her question until after John and I are done singing.

Why she didn't immediately call the Upland mental health department on her new co-worker who she caught singing into the work line insisting he was part of some live international broadcast is something I never fully figured out.

INTERIOR-The Mountain Goats backstage-Troubabdour-2002 or maybe it was 2003:

**John**: I wish I'd known you were here tonight. I would have brought you up for a duet of "Lonesome Surprise," just like we did on that Netherlands broadcast a few years back.

**You**: Next time, man.

**John**: Damn straight.

Great American Music Hall. San Francisco California. June 28, 2012.

"Before we go any further with tonight's set I got to make a quick call..." John says reaching into a pocket to grab his phone. The crowd erupts in laughter.

The crowd continues with their laughter as he proceeds to dial.

The audience's laughter begins to take on a dumbfounded tone. You can almost see a thought bubble forming above them *"My God he wasn't joking about having to make that call, was he?"*

"Hey. How's it going, Allen?" John says casually into the phone to scattered, somewhat perplexed applause.

John pushes the phone to the microphone.

"Pretty alright John…How are you?…And how are you San Francisco?"

San Francisco answers with a warm open roar.

John begins strumming the first few chords of "Lonesome Surprise."

"Allen, you still there?"

"Oh yeah…"

"Ladies and Gentlemen…for the first time singing from a stage since they put a new heart in him…Allen Callaci…"

The crowd on the other end is crackling and blazing like a wildfire as I get up off the sofa and start to sing and pace the carpeted floor in the tight-fitting surgical socks that grip my swollen ankles like a vise.

*Doctor, doctor…can you help me, please?*

I get goosebumps from the applause radiating out of the small plastic phone in the dark blue protector in the palm of my hand.

It's Karol's night to watch me. She is overly concerned about making any kind of noise that would thwart this musical moment. That's funny. She's seen enough Refrigerator shows to know musical perfection and professionalism are the last streets where I'll be found.

She'd never heard the story about John and me singing "Lonesome Surprise" from the Upland Library basement. And after all these years she thought she'd heard all my Upland Library stories. I guess I've still got some surprises left in me.

> Here's your lonesome surprise
> Lonesome surprise
> Lonesome surprise

"Thank you Allen, good night," says John as "Lonesome Surprise" wraps itself up. The audience's cheer swells, crests and crashes like a wave. John pauses to let the wave ride itself out.

"I really don't know what else I can play after that…" John tells the crowd as Karol helps me waddle my way back to the sofa.

"Lonesome Surprise" was written shortly after my dad passed.

It is a song about healing and continuing on.

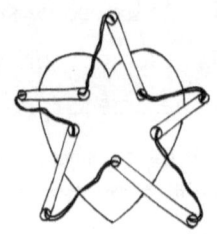

# THE JAMES TAYLOR SCARRED INTERSTATE

*I can't breathe…I can't breathe…I can't bre—*

The thought goes unfinished.

The conscious world collapses.

"I'm getting someone NOW!"

I didn't hear my sister's frantic cry as it filled the shoebox-sized room at San Antonio Community Hospital that day but I hear the echoes. Sometimes as I take my blood sugar and hope for a low reading. And sometimes when I wake up feeling a little more tired than the day before. And other times it's when I'm on the way to work, or while singing Otis Redding in the shower.

Rinse.

Heal.

Repeat.

    Rinse.

    Heal.

    Repeat.

Rinse.

Heal.

Repeat.

❦

*"No more than 5 minutes in the shower for the time being. Be careful 'round the chest area when you're in there. It's still so tender."*

That's what they told me at the clinical yesterday at Cedars.

After two-plus months of not being able to shower standing up I'll gladly take every minute in the shower they're willing to give me like a worm takes the rain.

A soft velour gray towel Jen's mom had lovingly sent me is laid out across the same white tiles I crashed down across a lifetime ago. It's the plushest, richest towel these tiles have ever been covered in. And unlike previous towels that have graced this bathroom floor, this one also happens to actually match the rest of the bathroom.

I tenderly lift each leg up and away from the soft gray velour and over the edge of the tub into the shower.

Does it hurt?

Yes.

Excruciatingly so?

No.

I mean yes.

Some new real estate has opened up beneath the showerhead since my last visit. The white plastic shower chair where I used to twist into a variety of yoga-like poses in order to wash myself has now been extracted from my bathroom like an infected tooth.

Slowly, nakedly I turn the water on.

TOOHOT!

 TOOHOT!

  TOOHOT!

Turn the knob more to the right.

Ok.

Better.

Much better.

The suds roll down. It's a baptism of sorts as the water rains down across the staples, the swollen pink scar and the small litter of glistening staples scattered across my chest like a small handful of dropped metallic seeds on this warm mid-June afternoon.

*Remember what they told you DO NOT let the water hit your chest*

*NO WATER ON THE CHEST…*

*NO WATER ON THE CHEST…*

The water descends and gradually creates a warm gentle pounding rhythm of its own.

And it is bliss.

Like being beneath a waterfall after 40 days in a desert.

The egg timer screeches.

It couldn't have been 5 minutes already.

It has.

♥

It will be another 5 weeks before I can go anywhere indoors other than the apartment. No walk-in movie theaters. No restaurants. No supermarkets. The new heart means having the immune system of an infant until August gets here.

When I was a child I longed to step on Venus and be surrounded by voluptuous, purple-skinned, three-breasted, women in chain-link bikinis.

Now I long only to step inside the frozen food section at Vons.

As I pull into the Vons parking lot the oldies station begins playing James Taylor's "Fire and Rain." I reach forward to take a quick Ali-esque jab at the dashboard radio preset button, but before I can fully connect the lush, plaintive melody has already blasted forth from the small plastic dashboard speakers like a nail bomb. I stay in the Vons parking lot motionless, flat, almost frozen. The cruel, soothing sounds of James Taylor swoops down, digs in its flesh-tearing claws and starts dragging me back.

You are an infant once again. Unable to dress yourself, feed yourself, hardly able to speak. You can't pee standing up. Your sheets are all changed for you. You even get sung to some nights as they tuck you in after they hear from your family how you sing in a band. They sing you everything from "You Light Up My Life" to traditional Filipino spirituals as they change your sheets and check your vitals.

"You like James Taylor much?"

You nod.

*I'm not the biggest James Taylor fan who ever walked the earth but James Taylor did have a cameo in one of my favorite episodes of* The Simpsons. *The one where Homer becomes an astronaut.*

"'Fire and Rain'? You know that one?"

You nod again.

"I love that one," he says. And starts right in.

You first heard "Fire and Rain" as a child from the duct-taped vinyl backseat of your mother's station wagon. It's a song you've heard more times than you've tied your shoes since then but one you've never really listened to till now. Sunny days without end. Pieces on the ground. Things to come.

The song is not the '70s feathered mustache/K-tel Records/soft-crusted oldie you'd always written it off as.

It is everything you are feeling but lack the physical voice to say.

…And you are so going to owe James Taylor an extended apology and two bottles of his favorite wine once you make it out of here.

"I brought you a gift," she says handing me a present decorated in zombie gift wrap.

"You didn't have to," I tell her.

"You be quiet. It's your Christmas gift," she says. "Open it."

I honor her request.

Beneath the Zombie wrapping paper lies a Simpsons T-shirt.

"Thanks so much for this," I say, proudly holding up the shirt.

"It's a medium. I know you're a medium," she says. She looks at me holding the shirt up against my tiny frame and quickly corrects herself. "Oh, I guess you're not a medium anymore are you?"

"…not really," I say smiling meekly. "…I've…uhm lost a lot of weight since the surgery…actually been a small since May …"

"Somehow I keep forgetting…" she says with a small pinch of sadness.

"It's a great shirt, Jen."

"I can exchange it if you like."

There's a small dry erase board that's updated constantly as if it were a scoreboard. The dry erase board tracks my daily intake of physical therapy exercise cycles, walks, and waters. I added the category of "ego massages" to the board the other day to liven it up. The new category has thus far gone criminally neglected.

The board makes for some pretty dry reading (unless you enjoy reading hashmarks). It rests on a shelf alongside some DVDs. Next to the board is a small stuffed bear in aqua colored hospital scrubs that was a gift from when I was at Cedars. Every time Pat swings by he looks over at the stuffed bear and cracks "I don't know, if I was a patient and my doctor was a grizzly bear in an ill-fitting surgical mask, I'd look into switching doctors."

"How is the healing is going?"

I get that a lot.

It is going.

What about you and your healing?

How is that going?

How are you holding up?

Can you even believe the shit we've pulled ourselves through?

Life.

Death.

Life again.

And yes, we exploded at times.

But all things considered how could we not have?

And things got said that should have gone unsaid.

And things went unsaid that should have been said.

And so I say this now:

Remember the old fable Androcles and the Lion? It begins with a poor young slave named Androcles pulling a thorn from a wounded lion's paw. The grateful lion thanks Androcles profusely for tending to his aching wound and vows to never forget Androcles' act of unfiltered kindness. They go their ways. They meet years later as Androcles is being thrown to a lion in a Roman Coliseum for a petty theft he has committed. The lion gets unleashed. He is the lion whom

Androcles had pulled the thorn from years earlier. He recognizes Androcles, and true to his word, spares Androcles his life. Empathy and gratitude rain down all across the kingdom. Androcles and the Lion stroll off, reunited, into that sunset of happily ever after.

Consider me a lion who has not forgotten your acts of kindness and sacrifice. So, which way to our sunset? We can take what we have left and begin things again with what isn't completely broken and what's still standing.

We have not been completely broken.

We are still standing.

# EXITS AND RE-ENTRANCES

"Are you ok back there?"

"I'm fine, Jen."

*The last time I was in Jen's Ascender we were speeding off to Urgent Care. The door handles and dashboard had not reeked of the fresh scent of Clorox lemon-scented hand wipes. I had been seated in the front seat not the back. There had been no thought about the damage the impact of an airbag might cause to my chest in case of a collision. There had been no secondhand pillow seat-belted securely across my chest.*

Jen looks worriedly into the rear view mirror at my pillow-insulated frame as we head towards the sci-fi club meeting at the library. Her look is the same one I used to have when I first started picking up Rael, when he was 5, and he'd be strapped in the back of my car.

"Jen, I'm fine."

"Nobody's saying you aren't," she says, glancing back again into the rear view mirror.

"Good, because I'm fine. I even made some chicken and broccoli for lunch today all by myself. Me, in the kitchen? Can you believe that? I can't. I think I deserve a couple points for that."

Jen proceeds to give me the response she has always given me whenever I've pressed her about how I think I'm deserving of a couple points for having accomplished some mundane task like feeding myself, vacuuming or scrubbing the bathroom floor until it shines like a lime-scented star.

"Well, you're not getting any points from me for doing something that you should be doing anyway."

She does not smile as she says this.

She never does.

I try not to smile either.

I do.

"I also finished up reading *Midsummer Night's Dream* for tonight." I say reaching for another quick distraction. "How about you? You finish?"

"I didn't have time."

"Well, don't be too hard on yourself," I jokingly chide her. "I've had a lot more down time than you've had lately."

"Not funny."

"No, probably not," I say, slightly adjusting the secondhand pillow seat-belted across my chest. "Probably not."

*And then there we are…gathered 'round the outside tables in the small patio area behind the library that Adam had reserved for us…copies of* A Midsummer Night's Dream *turned and opened to the stars…the crickets perfectly synced to the distant strains of "Follow the Yellow Brick Road" coming from* The Wizard of Oz *rehearsal going on next door at the Playhouse…all the world's a stage…we are merely players with our entrances and our exits and our re-entrances …*

A wireless microphone is in my hand and a small packet of almonds is tucked inside my jacket pocket as I await my entrance. Well, not technically an entrance, since I won't be able to enter anywhere outside my apartment for another month. It's more of an arrival. It is the library's annual celebration where library employees, members of the library foundation board and city council members come together to highlight the library's accomplishments over the past fiscal year.

The Rancho Cucamonga Public Library polo shirt I have on is the first shirt I've been able to pull over my head since early April. Pulling the shirt over my head and across my ultra-sensitive chest this morning wasn't that bad…no, actually, it was that bad…as I wriggled and winced my way into the shirt I felt like Houdini struggling to get out of a strait jacket.

A light year seems to have passed since I was last here. Stanchions encircle me. The stanchions have been placed behind Celebration Hall's exit door as a precaution to protect me from the danger of being pulled apart by 10,000 misty-eyed librarian embraces. I'm this year's surprise headliner. I wonder if this is how Elvis felt backstage at his 1968 Comeback special.

The back door to Celebration Hall cracks open a bit. Michelle pokes her head out and motions that my entrance is now only moments away.

*Keep it light. No need to make things any more emotionally draining than they already are.* I hear Margaret's unmistakable laughter coming through the barely cracked door like a buzzsaw. I've really missed that laugh. And that sounds like Linda…I think I also hear…

The *Star Wars* theme blasts in.

The exit doors to Celebration Hall get flung open. And there they are. Standing, and gasping. And crying. Even Isabel is crying and she just saw me two days ago.

"Why didn't you tell me you'd be making an appearance today?" she says, wiping away a tear. "I know you can't have hugs right now, but what about a strong swift kick to the gut for not telling me you'd be here?"

"I promised to keep it under wraps," I say. "We saw each other a few days ago when it was your turn to babysit me so I wasn't thinking this would shake you."

"You just weren't thinking," she says reaching into her purse for a Kleenex. "It's different seeing you here. Seeing you dressed in work attire. I feel like we should be walking back to your office right now and brainstorming plans for Superhero Saturday. And we're not."

"But we will be soon…we'll be back to being family Saturday planning machines…. although for the Hello Kitty family Saturday you might be on your own. They would take away my Mancard if I got too involved with that one."

"Stop trying to make me laugh."

They all swarm my direction. There's Carol who appreciates both the Beatles and Yoda as much as I do…there's Mandisa my sci-fi club co-founding cohort…there's Barb who has known me since I began as a part-time clerk 17 years ago…there's Lorena who I've mooched more Cheez-Its from than either of us would care to count…

There was a day back in April when it seemed like I'd be seeing them all again in a matter of days. And there was another day back in April where it seemed like I'd never see any of them again.

*Forget funny. Say something magical, something profound, something for the ages into that wireless mic. Stop drawing a blank. They're waiting. Say something. Anything…anything but some stupid shlocky cliché like "I've missed you all so much too …"*

I grasp the wireless mic a little tighter. Bring it in a little closer.

They are applauding wildly. All eyes on me. Time to own this moment with some cliché-free, incredibly graceful words of wisdom for the ages…drum roll please …

"I've missed you all so much too…"

## CHICKS DIG SCARS

HI ISABEL. SORRY FOR THIS LAST MINUTE TEXT. WENT TO URGENT CARE. ON MY WAY TO SAN ANTONIO. THEY THINK IT'S MY APPENDIX. CAN YOU BELIEVE THAT? CAN YOU PLEASE TELL WORK WHATS GOING ON AND THAT I PROBABLY WONT BE MAKING IT IN TOMORROW?

It's 2 pm. I'm not feeling any better than I was on the drive to work this morning. In fact I'm feeling worse. I only had a couple of bites of pizza for lunch. The pizza went down even worse than the strawberry smoothie I had earlier. I'm going home for the day.

*I've been so rundown all day. I was hoping I could shake it off by now but it's not going anywhere. If anything it's gotten worse since this morning. I never take sick days. They know I'm not cutting out early to go horseback riding at Disneyland.*

I tell my assistant Sean I'll be leaving for the day. I might not be in tomorrow as well. We'll see.

"Yeah, you're not looking well," he says.

"Why thank you for that analysis, Dr. Guerrero," I kid.

Sean is going to med school. One of his nicknames at work is

Dr. Guerrero. His other nickname is Russell due to his boyish resemblance to Russell, the overeager wilderness scout, from the Pixar film *Up*.

"Take care and no worries. Take a couple days if you really need them," Sean says. "I'll be here manning the fort till you get back."

"Thanks. Remember…no wild parties while I'm away." I grab my jacket from the back of the office chair and make my way to the office door. "See you in a few."

To the City of Rancho Cucamonga,

This letter is being submitted on behalf of heart transplant recipient Allen Callaci. Mr. Callaci may return to work at part time status with no restrictions in October 2012. He may return to work as a full time employee in March 2013.

Thank you,

Dr David Chang, MD

I'll be back to work by week's end. I've lost 25-plus pounds, maybe a little more than that, since I was last there. Most of the khakis and button down dress shirts that were my usual work attire now hang loosely off my body as if I were a skeletal coat-hanger.

*God. Look at me. I haven't been this thin since high school. It feels like I'm wearing a different man's clothes. My barber yesterday wanted to know where I've been and what my secret was to losing all this weight. How could I even begin to answer that in the time frame of a 25 minute haircut?*

After months of wearing loose-fitting Beatles T-shirts, denim shorts, and sweats it is time to dress like a "functioning adult" again.

My fashion has changed dramatically over the past seasons. Last winter my wardrobe consisted solely of khakis and long-sleeved button down shirts for workdays and shredded jeans and faded Batman or Charles Bukowski t-shirts for weekends.

*I could be such an inactive bum at times. Sleeping till 11 on weekends. By the time I showered, ate and dorked around online for a few hours it'd be 2 pm. 2 pm. Too late to go to the gym but just enough time to read an issue or two of* Man-Thing. *Ironically, had I spent my weekends doing three-mile mountain trail hikes at 6 am, my heart would have given out sooner from the stress and strain. I may have been the first person who ever put off a heart attack by spending weekends on his sofa reading dog-eared copies of* Man-Thing.

By spring my wardrobe had been reduced to a blue paper hospital gown and thigh-high compression socks. Compression socks are made from the strongest elastic which pushes and presses the blood from the feet to the heart to prevent clotting. If only they made—

*I would like to break in here with an urgent public service announcement expressing how I was being ironic in the comments above regarding reading dog-eared issues of* Man-thing *acting as a solid preventive measure against heart disease. Proper diet, regularly scheduled doctor visits and exercise are the real keys to preventing heart disease, not wasting weekends on the sofa reading rusted out copies of* Man-Thing.

*Always keep your medical card on you at all times.*

*Only you can prevent forest fires.*

*Be an organ donor.*

*Give a hoot, don't pollute.*

*Ok, now back to our regularly scheduled memoir already in progress...*

Summer brought sweat shorts and loose-fitting, short-sleeved, button-down shirts. The short-sleeved button shirts were necessary due to how tender my chest still was. The buttons on the shirt would feel like bee stings when they'd brush against my chest. I tried not to let myself imagine what a pullover shirt would feel like.

The button-down shirts were also necessary due to the ongoing hand tremors which combined with the inability to lift my hands completely over my head made it impossible to put on a pullover shirt. The physical therapist would come by once a week and have me stretch my arms towards the sky several times as the sky dangled just outside my reach.

"Back Allen Is" reads the thought bubble scrawled onto the Yoda poster that has been taped to the staff room door. It's been close to 6 months since I've seen the old staff room. Next week it'll be Halloween. I bask in the bold beauty and splendor of the Rancho Cucamonga public library staff room as if it were a picturesque Maui sunset.

The staff microwave which has diligently radiated God knows how many wrapped burritos and day old slices of pizza is right there.

The slow glowing vending machines hum the same vibrato song they have always hummed.

The copy of last week's issue of *Entertainment Weekly* featuring Mila Kunis' sexy green glare and the yellow brick headline "RETURN TO OZ" sits atop one of the small circular tables…

Back Allen Is.

…*I race back to the staff bathroom for the third time in less than an hour to collect myself. I let the faucet rain across my pale, shaky face, dab my red puffy eyes, and keep breathing in deeper and deeper until the tightening in my throat recedes. I softly repeat the same simple phrases to myself as if I were repeating Our Fathers and Hail Marys between the beads of a handmade rosary.*

*"It's going to get easier…it's going to get easier…it's going to get easier… things are going to get back to where they were… things are going to get back to where they were… things are going to get back to where they were …"*

"I brought a meatlover's pizza for your Welcome Back potluck," Adam dryly states. "Is that anything you can have?"

"I should probably stick to the carrot sticks and grilled chicken."

"Suit yourself," he says grabbing a slice and taking a bite. "You know what I'd do if I were you?"

"What would you do if you were me?"

"If I were you I'd never wear a shirt again…I'd be showing off my scar everywhere."

"Seriously?" I say, laughing so hard I'm almost snorting.

"Seriously…chicks dig scars."

The scar. It runs down the center of your chest like an interstate. It was hard to look down at it at first. You'd avoid eye contact with the bedroom mirror every morning as you threw on a fresh shirt. When you did catch a glimpse of it you'd quickly avert your eyes. As if you'd just looked directly into the sun. When you'd dream the scar was never there. When you'd awake it always was.

Scars heal. Slowly. But they heal. The chest hairs start coming back in. The soreness starts to dim. The scar begins to recede. To meld. To become a piece of you.

You look down at your scar…It's an interstate. An interstate that has taken you from where you've been to where you are.

It's ok to look down.

Chicks dig scars.

# AN UNEXPECTED JOURNEY

## I AM GOING TO MAKE IT THROUGH THIS YEAR IF IT KILLS ME…

"You know what all this has been like?" Dennis told me the other night. "Like dropping your last quarter into a pinball machine and magically winning another game on your last ball."

"This will mark the 4th time in the 6 years I've known you that you've moved, Jen. That's a lot. Like you're running away from something."

"Running away from something? And what exactly would it be I'm running from?"

"Yourself."

"Please. You've been saying these kinds of things a lot since the new heart."

These things the "new" heart says are the things the old heart wanted to say but never did. The conversations I've played out in my head 10,000 times are now being played aloud in real time.

"I'm not running away from anything," she says with an exasperated huff. "I've been up since 5 this morning. I don't need this. I'm perfectly happy with where I'm at," she says tensely.

"Are you?"

"Just drop it. I know things are different now for you but they aren't for me…"

"They are different for you too," I tell her. "You can't ride through the valley we just rode through and not be changed."

I think about a conversation I had with Isabel earlier at work. She asked if adapting back to normalcy after the transplant is similar to the process of adapting back to normalcy after a major loss. Yes. No. Not exactly. It's more like going through a loss and a rebirth simultaneously. Each moment becomes a moment to be held in a tight melancholy embrace simply because you are here to hold it.

"I really don't feel like talking about this right now."

"It's important to kick these things out into the open, Jen."

"But why now?"

"Why? Because now is all we've got."

"Hey, has the opening act already played?" you and Amy ask a middle-aged couple as you hurriedly rush through the cemetery gates. "We're running late."

"Nah, you ain't missed nothing," the stocky couple tell us. "…and if you've got to be late arriving anywhere it should be the cemetery, right?" Amy and I press onward in the direction of the stage as the couple's husky laughter trails off behind the tombstones.

I don't know how many times I've seen the Mountain Goats play. More than I can count on my hands and toes combined. I've seen them play everywhere from Paris, France to Kristi's mom's North Upland living room. I have never seen them play a graveyard.

The Mountain Goats are playing the Hollywood Forever Cemetery. It's two weeks outside of Christmas. Mel Blanc, the voice of

Bugs Bunny and Marvin the Martian, is buried here. So are Johnny and Dee Dee Ramone. The ashes of an old friend of John's rests here as well. John had texted earlier in the day about what a rough show this was going to be.

The rain has not let up all day.

"Turn back or keep pressing forward?" Amy had asked earlier as we hit West Covina and the rain tap-danced heavily across the windshield.

"Keep pressing forward."

"I knew you were going to say that. That's what you always say."

  Count a couple of stray hopes out loud,
  May their numbers one day be increased.
    Plug a night light in.
    Leave the porch light on.

A warm six-string rhythmic glow is cast from the stage to the farthest corners. Hundreds of basking bodies absorb the rays and raise their voices. A light strong enough to cut across every rain-soaked, cold granite headstone has been lit.

"I'm so glad you were there telling me to push forward and not turn back the whole ride out," Amy whisper/shouts to me mid-song.

"I'd like to dedicate this next one to my good friend Allen who had a heart transplant earlier this year. I know he's out there somewhere tonight. For those who don't know, Allen sings in a band called Refrigerator and just happens to be one of the all-time greatest singers ever ..."

John and his grand proclamations ...

"Thanks Johhhhhn!" I holler out from somewhere alongside the right hand side of the stage. It's hard to believe that out of the two of us Amy was the one who's been drinking and not me.

John chuckles onstage. "That's good. You're here. You're here... alright now let's go!"

The first dizzying, triumphant notes of "This Year" ring out. I had texted John earlier telling him how this song had become my anthem over the summer, my constant companion over the last few months helping hold me together through each color-coded pill, mealtime injection and scarred, strained step:

One. Two. Three. Four. Lift.

FUarrrrrrrrrghhhhhhhCK

One. Two. Three. Four. Lift again.

*There will be feasting and dancing in Jerusalem next year, I am going to make it through this year if it kills me*

It's been more than a year since I last saw John in the flesh. So much has gone on since we last spoke in July for the phoned-in performance of "Lonesome Surprise" at his San Francisco show. What is there to say?

The set is finished. The amps get wheeled back. The guitars go back in their cages.

"God damn, it's good to see you!" John says punching his arms in the air and running up to give me a monster bear hug.

I grit my teeth and clench my fingers to keep from crying.

"You too, man. You too."

… there is nothing else to say.

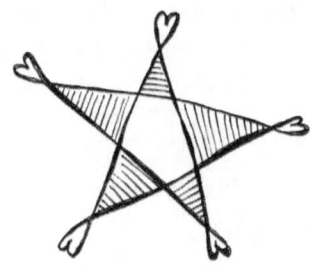

## SPIRIT IN THE NIGHT

"Oh my God, it's you," Dr. Wang exclaims as a smile spills from beneath his surgical mask. "It's you! I'm sorry for not recognizing you."

Why would he recognize me? The last time Dr. Wang and I saw each other I had on a surgical mask as well. I was 25 pounds heavier. My glasses were off. And my chest was open.

Dr. Wang reaches across the counter and touches my shoulder as if to make sure it's me and not an apparition. "You were sick. So, so sick…I remember …"

Dr. Wang clutches his forehead, takes a few extended breaths of deep concern and looks down. He tells Dennis and Loretta to start making calls. Start making them now. It could be a matter of days. A transplant is the only chance now. An almost nonexistent chance but the only one there is. They have done all they can at San Antonio. He will be contacting Cedars-Sinai.

Loretta breaks down.

*This isn't happening.*

*This isn't happening.*

*This isn't happening.*

<small>*This isn't happening.*</small>

Dr. Wang looks back down and clutches his forehead a little tighter. "I will send a prayer. I don't know him, but I look at all the love that surrounds him and know that this is a good man."

I hand Dr. Wang the small gift-wrapped box of assorted chocolates.

"Happy Holidays, Dr. Wang."

There is a brief moment of warm silence as he looks down at the box of chocolates.

"Thank you …" he says as he takes the box. He closes his eyes for a few lingering seconds. "So good to see you. So, so good to see you …"

Bruce Springsteen's hoarse voice fills the arena. I've got a small plastic cup of premium wine in my hand. Jen has a cranberry juice and vodka in hers. I waited 25 minutes in line for the small plastic cups we hold in our hands. Nothing compared to the 7 months that have passed since Bruce was last in town.

The last time Bruce played here I was half conscious in a San Antonio Hospital bed:

"I'm sorry, Jen."

"Sorry about what?"

"Right now, we should be excitedly getting ready for the Springsteen show…not here in this cramped hospital room."

"Will you be quiet? Bruce Springsteen is the least of my concerns right now."

"I know. I just really wanted to go."

"I know you did. So did I," she says with a sad sympathetic smile. "We'll catch him next time…next time."

I took Jen to her first Bruce show. "I'll go," she said "but mainly to hear 'Glory Days.' He'd better do 'Glory Days.'" He didn't. She described the show on the ride back home as cleansing and uplifting, like going to church. Although she still couldn't believe he could play for over three hours and not do "Glory Days."

"This next one is about ghosts," Bruce rasps into the mic. "The people you've lost but still feel walking along beside you."

I've seen Springsteen a dozen times. The first time with my father back in '84. After years of lovingly and begrudgingly taking Dennis and me to one bad Twisted Sister or Mötley Crüe concert after another it was nice to see him smiling and bobbing his head at a show as Bruce belted out "Cover Me." I remember thinking how I hadn't seen him that happy at a show since Elton John at Dodger Stadium back in '75.

"We're going to send this one from our ghosts to your ghosts," Bruce announces as the first tear-stained notes of "My City of Ruins" ring out.

I can sense the presence of my father in the aisles of the concrete arena. I can see him hustling to make it back to his seat as he steadily balances the nachos and the sodas loaded in his hands. He doesn't want to miss a note. I don't want him to either.

I glance towards Jen as the last strains of "My City of Ruins" reach towards the roof. My fingers shake as I raise the clear plastic cup of wine to my trembling lips like an altar boy as Bruce kicks into "Spirit In The Night."

"I'm here for you Johnny H. I'm here, man."

"Johnny H" being local blues legend John Harrelson.

"Here" being the rehab clinic where Johnny H was moved after being released from San Antonio Hospital a few weeks earlier.

His room at San Antonio had been next door to the room I had been placed a year earlier. He is fast asleep as I enter his room with a Keith Richards autobiography tucked under my arm. He is wrapped...breathing heavy...

*...I look down at him there...I hear the howl of his voice and the way it touched the moon on a night more than two decades down...my father had just passed...Dennis, Loretta, and I had recently moved into his old house...fresh painful reminders of loss on every wall, mantelpiece, and picture frame...and there was Johnny H that night strumming and growling...caught between the stars and the dead backyard grass of my father's house...his songs touching down like a healing balm to a burn... you're gonna make it the fuck out of here John...you've got to make it the fuck out of here ...*

Only the soft light of the muted TV breaks up the room's darkness. I take a seat next to his bed and quietly read a few decadent passages from the Keith Richards book aloud. Not loud enough to wake Johnny H but loud enough for him to know that a voice is there.

The recording studio is a little chilly this November Sunday. November Sundays can be like that. Adam Lipman and I are finally getting around to recording the songs we talked about recording early last spring.

"I loved the backing vocals you laid on my last record. I need to kidnap you someday and have you sing my entire catalog," Lipman joked.

"You know that's not a bad idea," I answered. "We should do it. You don't even need to kidnap me."

"Serious?"

"Serious."

"When can we do it?"

"I don't know. We'll figure it out. We've got time."

"Yeah, nothing but..."

A few weeks after that conversation I collapsed in an unconscious pile across white, cold, linoleum bathroom tiles.

*And a few weeks after that my heart would stop and …*

*… no, don't even go there …*

Steve Folta is engineering today's recording.

"Can you step up to the mic so we can get some vocal levels," he asks.

"Ok," I answer as I secure the headphones and try to breathe life into the lyrics carefully balanced on the music stand in front of me. I take a step and a long, deep breath into the silence waiting to be filled.

"We're rolling," says Steve.

I take another deep breath in and start painting in the silence.

> I miss you when you are asleep.
> So don't be angry
> If I wake you up
> And kiss you goodnight again

If this were a fairy tale it would end with my being awoken with a kiss.

This is life, not some paint-by numbers fairy tale.

"I remember telling my co-worker Olivia how I kissed you on the forehead while you lay there unconscious. And how you suddenly opened your eyes," Jen is telling me some months later. "She joked how my kiss had brought you back from the dead."

*... And so they all lived on happily ever after in the face of their losses and pains and aches and disappointments...because they were all still there to hurt, and to suffer, to grow and live on ...*

# HERE COMES THE SUN

The thin catheter with a small grasping hook attached to the end of it digs its way through my neck and worms its way towards my heart. "Now turn your head all the way to the left. Good. This is going to sting," they tell me, like they have at every biopsy, as the catheter begins its mission, collecting cells from the surface of my heart like a guided unmanned space probe.

*It's like being stung by a 3-pound wasp as they inject you with a sedative to numb the neck before putting the catheter in. It pinches like a lobster as the catheter begins to worm its way down through your neck towards your heart. And then it burns for a brief moment the way that pressing a finger down on dry ice does.*

"Fields of Gold" by Sting plays softly in the background. It's from a CD mix another biopsy patient had brought in consisting of nothing but Sting songs. They amusingly entitled the CD *This is going to Sting*. God, I wish I would have thought of that title. They told me awhile back I could bring in a CD mix of my own one of these days if I liked. I never did. I honestly don't know if even my music obsessed self could come up with something as clever as *This is going to Sting*. Rush "Closer to the Heart" followed by Janis Joplin's "Take Another Little Piece of my Heart"?

The collected cells from the biopsy are taken to the lab and analyzed to make sure that the body is not rejecting the new heart.

I close my eyes and try to tune out Sting, and the catheter digging into the side of my neck, and think of a favorite Beatles song instead. My arteries are a little dry this morning so it takes a little more time than usual to find the right spot to press in the catheter. That's alright. I still haven't settled on which Beatles song to throw on the turntable stored inside my mind.

"You got the right mindset," Heart Family Volunteer Bill told me earlier as he escorted me back. "Some of the people I take back for their biopsy complain about the traffic or the fasting or having to come so early…they forget."

"Forget what?"

"To be grateful to be alive."

The heart skips a few palpitations as the catheter scratches the heart's surface. It feels like my entire chest is sucking in a few deep breaths as the palpitations skip and Sting croons on around me about a brand new day.

"…it is Monday April 1st 10 am. We are about to begin the biopsy on patient Allen Callaci by entering through the right side of the patient's neck …"

"Come Together"…"Golden Slumbers"…"Something"…I mentally make my way through most of *Abbey Road* as the biopsy continues… even "Maxwell's Silver Hammer," which I've never really cared for.

"Take a deep breath and then hum," I'm instructed as the catheter gently begins its journey back. After close to a year of weekly, and then monthly biopsies, this will be the LAST of the biopsies. THE LAST.

I hum "Here Comes the Sun" as the catheter slowly gets tugged out from the right side of my neck for the last time.

It's the first day of daylight saving time. There is still some light left as we begin to load in and carry the banged-up, stickered guitar cases and beat-up amps up the concrete steps into the darkly lit American Legion hall. As I enter, the strains of Dobie Gray's "Drift Away" shoot through my faded, black Sandman "You get what anybody gets - you get a lifetime" T-shirt and hit me squarely in the chest.

My eyes adjust from the sunlight to the dimly lit hall and the handful of old soldiers scattered around the bar and pool table. The American Legion was founded in the early 1900s by veterans returning home from World War I. The numerous Legion Halls that have been established since the Legion's inception are places for vets to gather collectively to forget their battles and their scars. To heal. To reconnect.

We will be going on less than two hours from now for our first live show since the transplant.

Dobie Gray continues crooning on behind me about grabbing that beat and getting lost in the rock 'n' roll.

"Did you talk to Rolo about collecting donations for the Cedars-Sinai Heart Research Institute at the show this weekend?"

"Yeah, he's completely onboard. He can provide a table but we need to provide someone to staff it."

"Ok," Dennis asks with his trademark dark sarcasm, "who loves us but hates our music that would want to do this now that Mom is gone?"

"Thanks to Liz Gilbert for opening. So good to be here at Legion Hall. Thanks for having us. Hope we're not too out of place here. I'm a librarian by day, not a veteran, although I was once a member of the KISS Army."

❦

"How you doing kid? I hope you haven't read this one yet," James says holding up a copy of *Kiss and Sell: The Making of A Supergroup*.

You shake your head 'no'. You'd say more but it hurts to speak. You smile as you take in the cover. There they are. The heroes of your youth…the spaceman, starchild, the cat, and of course Gene Simmons the fire breathing, blood spewing bat demon.

You're still not all there. But James is here. You, James and Gene Simmons. This is some rock 'n' roll quality time. You met James 15-plus years ago when you opened a show for his band, Yo La Tengo, at the Whiskey a Go Go. You played like a sloppy, unrehearsed, out of tune shame that night, but only because you were.

James is still James. Sports, Simpsons, and rock 'n' roll. He flew all the way in from Brooklyn to be here today.

*I can't believe James flew all the way in from Brooklyn. I remember Dennis saying he was flying in the other day but, as with so much else these past few days, I couldn't tell if that conversation was real or imagined. The line between what is real and what is imagined has become dangerously thin these days. The other night I could have sworn there was a fluorescent purple and green moss crawling across the ceiling.*

"It's the most hilarious book," James continues. "Want me to read a little bit from it?"

You nod.

James begins to read the tale of rock 'n' roll excess covered in Kabuki makeup. The book has everything…guns, money, drugs, Diana Ross, and Cher.

As James continues reading you notice the bright blue VISITOR bracelet wrapped around his wrist.

"Let me find the part where KISS makes their first million and Peter Criss asks if he now gets to go to this secret island he's heard of that's filled with nothing but millionaires…it's just hilarious."

"I see they gave you a backstage pass," you gurgle and point towards his VISITOR bracelet.

"Yeah…Thanks for getting me on the list, man," James heartily laughs. "Think next time you could get me a plus one?"

"Heart Like a Starfish" is the last song listed on the setlist.

I wrote "Heart Like a Starfish" in 1992. I still have no idea what the song's about exactly but I can tell you that the title was inspired by something I once read about how a heart, like the leg of a starfish, can be broken and then re-grown.

"You love my brother, don't you, Jen?" asks Dennis.

She doesn't answer. She looks down. A nervous giggle flutters from her lips and across the hospital waiting room as if it were a moth looking for a light.

"You don't have to answer."

She doesn't.

It is Saturday. And it is June. Jen and I are there on my 300 dollar sofa watching the made-for-HBO movie *Hemingway and Gellhorn*. It will be another 6 weeks, 2 days, 6 hours, 37 minutes and 12 seconds before I will be able to spend a Saturday independent of the 300 dollar sofa.

"There's nothing to writing," Hemingway bellows at us from the screen. "All you do is sit down at your typewriter and bleed."

"You think that's true, Mr. English Major?" Jen turns and asks.

"Seems fair enough. Who am I to argue with Hemingway?" I shrug. "Sometimes writing can make others bleed as well."

"I have no idea what you're even talking about," she laughs.

"I read the pages you sent me…I could really hear your voice as I read it…you need to do something with this . . I'm not just saying this because I know you either…"

"I know you're not, Bubba. You've been one of my toughest critics since you were a 16-year-old student worker of mine at the La Verne law library and proofreading my papers for me…"

"Best and worst job ever…" she laughs and shakes her head. "And by the way, you do know that you can call me Emily instead of Bubba now that we are no longer surrounded by a million other co-workers also named Emily?"

"I know, Bubba…I'm just set in my ways…I'm still trying to come to terms with the fact that you're now old enough to drink."

"I knew you were going to say that," she laughs again. "…the publisher I work for is a children's publisher but I'd be happy to help with the book…send you a list of publishers and agents I think might be a good fit …"

"That'd be such a help…I know less about the publishing world than I do the female mind …"

"Speaking of the female mind…the one thing I think the book needs is to be clearer about the relationship between you and Jen …"

"I don't know, Bubba. It's complicated. It's like what Princess Leia tells Vader about holding onto power: holding onto power is like holding onto sand. The tighter you clench your fist to hold onto it the more it slips through your fingers. Love and the people you love can be like that too."

I had a name

I had a place

But like the clothes I wear

The holes grow everywhere

Til it's like having nothing at all

Here's your lonesome surprise

Lonesome surprise

I take out my cell phone and give John a call from the stage of the American Legion Hall for another a phoned-in duet of "Lonesome Surprise." For this go round, our roles have been reversed. It is John singing from his home and me singing from the stage.

There are no surgical compression socks involved whatsoever.

From: John Darnielle
Sent: Monday, March 11, 2013 9:53 AM
Re: American Foreign Legion Lonesome Surprise sing-a-long
was it really ok? I wish you could have been here in the room, it felt so sweet - sweet in a big way, sweet rich amazing - to be standing here singing that song
SO MUCH LOVE!-John

I like the way you keep your room

just the way you left it

even when you're here

Songs that were written a decade or more ago feel as if they were written earlier this afternoon as we make our way down the setlist. As I sing the words they feel like they now mean what they were always meant to mean. The simple two word ending refrain of "One of Everything" is no longer sung with a lonely sense of resignation but with a sense of hard-earned celebration as a few scattered voices in the crowd sing it along with us:

> YOU'RE HERE
>
> YOU'RE HERE
>
> YOU'RE HERE

Wow,
I am still soaking in last night. Relishing in it actually. I can't take it all in.
I can't take it!
Seeing all of you together again... the soul that came through ... the connection you have with each other through your music... the lyrics that took on new meaning...the way your music really tells the stories...and the way you have to dig through the metaphors and play on words to experience it, gets richer and richer for me. It seems like every song speaks of last year. You could feel the heart and spirit in the room last night.

I wanted to scream out 'we did it!! We all did it!! Allen is here!' It was a victory celebration! I am so blessed to have both of you on this journey, and even if I wasn't your sister, I would be in awe of the men you have become. And I am.

What a monumental night. When Allen sang one of the new ones about

'everything that's been done to me'…I nearly lost it, and when I looked up, Amy Maloof had tears streaming down her face too. We looked at each other and she smiled and pointed at me…she was right there with me.
Crazy, crazy night. There were days I never thought I would see Refrigerator again. And so many others felt the same way…I kept watching Daniel and Nacho … remembering how faithful they have been and the true connection you guys all have.
Last night felt so raw and so true and so ecstatic all at the same time! You two on the floor singing, John Darnielle, Dennis bouncing off the walls antagonizing the audience. (still got your moves, bro)……. Allen singing tourist through the crowd, incredible…Leonard Cohen…all my personal favorites … Just surreal to have Harmonie singing all the words and dancing, sitting at the front with Henry and Mia…all the donations pouring in…Watching Rael really enjoying it and smirking at the Leonard Cohen jokes…Catherine and I exchanging knowing glances…. what a perfect way to begin the rest of the story………….
Thank you for last night, it was a healing balm for my heart
I love you,
Loretta

"Helloooooooo Pomona!!!" I bellow into the mic. "I've never been so happy to utter that phrase so I'm just gonna go ahead and utter it again…HELLOOOOOOO POMONA…we love you!!!"

The first chiming notes of "Bicycle" float off into the ether. I run right off after them…

"I look around at all the different people gathered here from all the different corners of your life and I think this isn't like being at a Refrigerator show at all; this is more like being at your wedding…" Loretta observed.

Where Loretta sees weddings, Dennis sees funerals. "This was like playing the best funeral ever…" He's beaming after the show. "A funeral without a body."

We played our first show in nearly two years last night in our adopted hometown of Pomona, the place where Refrigerator began and never left. Loretta's daughter Harmonie & our youngest, Henry, worked the front door (with oversight from Catherine & Cousin Melody) and gathered donations for the Cedars-Sinai heart transplant research foundation. It was overwhelming to see all of our friends and family last night, divorced from waiting rooms, fluorescent overheads, mirror mopped tile floors and uncomfortable waiting room chairs. Things go wrong all of the time, and even the largest of heartaches and sickness and the passing of loved ones always leaves our family gifts, many of which are to be discovered weeks months hours and days after the fact; the closeness and the kindness and the sweetness that is brought out by those that are both near and far to us. Last night was all of these things making themselves known. Sending all of our love to you for all of the many, many things you all did for my brother. Let's get together real soon, I owe you a drink.
Signing off,
Dennis

The first song on the last Refrigerator CD that was recorded before the transplant was called "Be Positive."

The small circular sticker stuck at the end of your Cedars-Sinai hospital bed reads "B-Positive." "B-Positive" Loretta says reading the sticker. "Could you please thank whoever it was who put such a strong positive message at the foot of my brother's bed. You have all been so great."

"That's sweet of you," the nurse says smiling and shaking her head. "B-Positive is actually his blood type. But I like how you think."

"Uhm… this next one is called 'Be Positive' which I recently learned also happens to be my blood type."

"Of course it is! …" a voice from the back bellows.

If your book of strings gets misplayed<br/>
I will bend it back into key<br/>
Spend the free time that I find somewhere<br/>
On a cure or something …

Close to 500 dollars is raised at the door. Our portion is donated to the Cedars-Sinai Heart Institute.

Hey be positive<br/>
See this isn't over<br/>
Hey be positive<br/>
See this isn't over<br/>
Hey…hey…hey …

The eclipse that occurred on the day my new heart was put in was the first annular eclipse of the 21st century. An annular eclipse differs from a standard eclipse in that the sun does not go completely dark. Only the center goes dark. The circumference of the sun can still be seen blazing like a bright orange stain left from the bottom of a cosmic coffee cup on a pitch black table cloth. The overhanging darkness gets ringed by the light.

I find my way from the Legion Hall to the Corolla. It is the first day of daylight saving time. An extra hour of daylight has been granted to be made the most of. To be danced with, sung to, captured and then set free.

You get what anybody gets - you get a lifetime.

## THERE AND BACK AGAIN

Gandalf: You'll have a tale or two to tell of your own when you come back.

Bilbo Baggins:...Can you promise that I will come back?

Gandalf: No. And if you do...you will not be the same.

Today marks 6 months since the transplant took place. As Loretta and I pull into Cedars for my clinical I look up to see what film my favorite metaphorical movie billboard has for me today. The one I used to turn my under-stimulated, over-analytical mind over to on my daily walks across the glass encased bridge at Cedars. When you're a Southern California native you don't look for signs reading tea leaves, you look for them in monster-sized movie billboards. I hope it's not *Skyfall*. How terrifying would that be?

As the billboard comes ever so slowly into view, a sense of relief, and self-loathing for placing such stock in airbrushed movie ads, arises. *The Hobbit: An Unexpected Journey*... an unexpected journey... yeah, yeah, ok, that fits.... .that works...of course...an unexpected journey...after all this, what else could it have possibly been?

Why the *Hobbit: An Unexpected Journey* billboard should bring such a sense of comfort and relief to a college-educated man living in the 21st century I couldn't tell you.

I can only tell you that it does.

"I was so terrified to see you that first time. I didn't know what to expect. I was getting all the updates from Loretta on my phone…I pictured you so frail and weak with all those tubes and IVs and…I was scared…scared you'd feel how scared I was and you'd get that scared too…I prepped myself mentally about what might be behind that door before I entered your room…I took some extended deep breaths…and there you were…and your hair was brown and thick with curls…not the thinning graying threads it had been for as long as I'd known you…and there was so much more color in your face…and you were smiling…you looked better than I'd ever remembered seeing you …"

```
From: dennis callaci
Sent: Monday, December 17, 2012 9:18 PM
Allen,
```
Everything is bleeding into everything else, this is a missive I had to get out after watching a documentary about John Harrelson this past weekend. He has gone through similar trials which made me think of you.
Even after all that you & I have done & said, there is still so much more that is unsaid that has meant the world to me & I know to you as well.  We are each other's heroes in this world, and how many people can say that about their brother or sister or partner?
I am so humbled to have one of each, all I can do is hope to share my wealth with the people that I love or that I have not loved enough. There are so many lyrical moments delivered by you on the Adam Lipman recording from last month that are tied into the struggle of this year that it makes my head reel.  Listening again tonight to

those recordings, an easy & carefree weekend of recording does not mean that the work done was easy or carefree. It is clear to me that this world is a Rorschach test, that we choose to see things in a light that is reflected from us.

I flash back sometimes to your being so swollen in that bed after they had opened & closed your chest 3 times in as many days that I didn't recognize you. What kind of fucked up lottery did we win that Loretta, Catherine, you & I see this year as one of the best years of our lives? In our sorrow, we often say that we just can't get over/believe what is before us. How wonderful that in our joy and jubilation we can say the same thing in a totally different key. I love you so much. Thank you for fulfilling the promise of not giving up. Christmas is weeks away but it has already presented itself to me.

Love you,
Dennis

### The Twelve Days of Transplant (sung to the tune of the 12 Days of Christmas)

*As originally performed at the 2012 Cedars-Sinai Holiday Celebration*

On the first day of transplant I woke up groggilly

For a new heart is inside of me

On the second day of transplant the surgeons said to me-

Keep those coughs-a-coming

On the third day of transplant-doctors watching me

Take your medications

On the fourth day of transplant rehab starts for me

Walk in the hallways

On the fifth day of transplant my family came to me

# WILD MOOD SWINGS*

On the sixth day of transplant another agony
Hospital food is boring
On the seventh day of transplant a bronch or biopsy
No complications
On the eighth day of transplant escape at last for me
Where is that clinic?
On the ninth day of transplant my energy is back
Thanks to the steroids!
On the tenth day of transplant nurses said to me
Stick to your diet
On the eleventh day of transplant my test results are back
Hurray! No rejection!
On the twelfth day of transplant the joy is hitting me
My new life is beginning ...

"Hey, where are you going?" Loretta asks as I get up from our table.

"I just saw Dr. Ramzy. I'm going to go thank him for all he has done and wish him a happy holiday."

"Yeah, you definitely need to go over and do that."

I do.

*Dr Ramzy was on the phone every hour checking in on my progress after performing my 8-hour LVAD surgery. Of the 5 times I was opened*

---

\* "Thank you so much for not having wild mood swings," Loretta whispers to me when they reach this line. "They warned us they would come but they never did. I don't know how you did it. Maybe you're some kind of secret Zen master."

up that time had been the trickiest.

They have rooms at Cedars-Sinai where doctors can rest on site in case they are needed in the hours immediately following a critical surgery. It was one of these rooms that Dr. Ramzy was staying in the night after he performed my LVAD surgery. I was losing too much blood. Dr. Ramzy had hoped the LVAD would be enough, but too much blood had been lost. The blood-thinners I was on to prevent clotting led to more blood loss than they had hoped. An RVAD (Right Assist Ventricular Device) was going to be needed as well.

Dr. Ramzy was rushed over from his site room. He had already performed the 8-hour LVAD surgery and now would be performing the 4-hour RVAD surgery. The blood running through my heart would be rerouted through the heart-lung machine once again. The machine would be asked to take over for my heart and lungs for the length of another surgery. Another incision through the breastbone would be made.

Dr. Ramzy stoically enters the Cedars-Sinai waiting room. He motions to Dennis and Loretta.

"…We've done all we can… It is all on him from here on out … how his body endures after losing all that blood and being opened up so many times in such a short period … there is some hope … but I'm afraid it's a slight … "

Dennis and Loretta hang silent in the still of the waiting room. They hold on to one another as if they were both made of Velcro. Dr. Ramzy returns his sleep-deprived self back to the operating room.

I finally spot Dr. Ramzy in the far corner. A few of his former patients surround him giving him shaky, misty-eyed handshakes and urging him to have a happy holiday. I work my way over and wait my place in line. Darlene Love's "Christmas (Baby Please Come Home)" soulfully rains down inside the Universal Hilton ballroom. When I finally reach him and go to shake his hand I am overwhelmed by the thought that the hand I am shaking is a hand that once held the heart that now beats on inside of me.

"Thank you, Doctor," I say. "I wouldn't be here celebrating this holiday without you. So, thank you."

He nods his head humbly at my gratitude.

He is one of the top transplant doctors in the country but looks young enough that if you were a bartender and he tried to order a mojito you would immediately ask to see some ID.

"This is my first time being at one of these celebrations," he tells me.

"Yeah...mine too," I crack.

He pats me on the shoulder. A minor smile crosses his shaking head. It's the same smile he flashed earlier at the holiday celebration when Dr. K made him stand up as he introduced him from the stage. "And a nice hand for Dr. Ramzy. For all you ladies out there, he's single!"

Loretta remembers one of the nurses telling her, "Dr. Ramzy says he's single but he's not. He is married to what he does."

Back at our table Loretta desperately grasps for a napkin to wipe her teary eyes with.

A projected slide show of the 91 patients who had transplants at Cedars-Sinai the past year begins. The slides of smiling surviving faces, accompanied by Louis Armstrong's "What a Wonderful World," fall and dissolve into one another like snowflakes making their way towards the earth.

I learned in 1st grade that each snowflake is unique. Each changes in shape and design as it falls from the clouds and gets exposed to the fluctuating temperatures the world throws its way.

Cut to: A woman in her 40s in a white stretch leotard doing a handstand...a man in his late 50s grasping a gigantic trout with both his hands...A grinning red-haired 30-year-old posing next to a screaming yellow motorcycle...a woman my age in a bright green sweater clutching her chubby-cheeked young daughter...and a guy who could be my dead-ringer wearing khaki shorts and brandishing a blue lightsaber from some far-off distant galaxy that looks suspiciously like my living room …

None of the faces from the slides would be here right now had we been born a few decades earlier. Not landed where we landed, when we landed, and not been fortunate enough to be surrounded by those we were surrounded by.

The last face fades.

The light comes back.

The warm growl of Louis Armstrong plays out across my mind as I exit the celebration and head towards the car. Harmonie comes racing after me.

"Are you sad you didn't win anything tonight in the raffle, Uncle Allen?" she asks. "I bet you really would have loved those Dodgers tickets."

The gravelly voice of Louis Armstrong continues ringing in the back of my mind as I throw an arm around her.

"It's all ok," I tell her. "I won big all year long."

# ACKNOWLEDGMENTS ETC...

Perhaps the most difficult page of this book to write is this one. Trying to quell that constant nagging fear you will inadvertently leave someone out who helped hold you up and pull you through some pretty icy hours. There were so many. So many that the staff at San Antonio had to ask Loretta and Dennis to relay a message to them all to stop calling as they were tying up all the hospital phone lines. How do you begin to pay that kind of debt of gratitude back? Part of me feels like I should simply leave a blank space on this acknowledgements page for anyone I may have left out to fill their name in _____. That'd be the coward's way out. I will leave a blank space just in case. Thank you all from the bottom of both my old heart and the new.

Dr. Wang at San Antonio Community Hospital.

The miracle workers at Cedars-Sinai: Danny Ramzy, MD, PhD, FRCSC; Jon Kobashigawa, MD; Michelle Maya Kittleson, MD; David H. Chang, MD; and Merlinda, Gillian, Anna, and a nursing team beyond compare.

Dennis Callaci and Loretta James. FOR EVERYTHING.

Jennifer Burnette for everything else.

Amy Maloof for the Amy-azing cover art and illustrations.

Marc "Cappy" Campos for the author shot.

Catherine Guffey, Rael, Harmonie, and Henry. Chris Wochosky, Eileen and Melodi McMillan, Joe, Bill, and Charles Callaci. Pat and Lisa Jankiewicz and family, Bob and Karol Almanzar and family, Isabel Guzman, Jarad Arbuckle, Becky Lizama, Allison Evans for suggesting a nonlinear approach, Heather Cousin, Cara Graf, Christopher and Lisa Delgadillo and the entire Sex and Blessings book club, Kristi Engle, David and Joanne Austin and family, Suzanne Burnette and George McMurray, Joan Brown and the City of Hope all-star dancers, Phyllis and Jerry Carriere, Carlos Valdez and Liz Perpetua, Chris Castillero and family, Antonio Abbondanza, Jennifer Delgado, Kevin Powell, Dwight Gilbert, Kirk McConnell and the Infinite Dominions speculative fiction book club.

Bandmates in arms: Chris Jones and Daniel Brodo.

My rock 'n' roll friends: Chris Knox, Steve Folta, Joel Huschle, Nathan Wilson, Adam Lipman, James McNew, Georgia Hubley and John Darnielle.

May the force be with you: Shawn "Obi-Wan" Crosby, Scott Allen, Inland Empire Fan Force, Rebel Legion, Dark Empire Radio, Mandalorian Mercs, Mary Franklin and Lucasfilm.

Robert Karatsu and Michelle Perera and the ENTIRE staff of the Rancho Cucamonga Public Library: Barb Tuckerman, Vivian Garcia, Adam Tuckerman, Lorena Paz, Renee Tobin, etc…file under "appreciated more than you'll ever know."

Kristina Allende, Gary Enke, Kim Garcia, my Freshman Composition class of spring 2012 and the entire Mt. SAC English Department.

And final thanks to Mandisa Tutt for her encouragement and guidance in putting this all together and being the first one brave enough to wade through it with me, Emily Feinberg for being brave enough to be the second, Ira Kaplan for the final edit, David Allen for the one after that, and Mark Givens for running with it from there.

An exclusive 3-track EP is available with the purchase of this book. Songs include:

- **Heart Like a Starfish**

- **Be Positive**

    Recorded at the first Refrigerator post-transplant performance - more a victory lap than a rock n roll show. Refrigerator features Daniel Brodo on bass, Allen Callaci on vocals, Dennis Callaci on guitar and backing vocals, and Chris Jones on drums. Recorded live at Pomona American Legion Hall, Pomona CA, March 10, 2013

- **Lonesome Surprise**

    Incredibly rough and ragged version of the Refrigerator song as sung through an old flip phone to an incredibly loving, patient and forgiving Mountain Goats audience. It marked the first time Allen sang in front of an audience post-transplant surgery. This track features John Darnielle on guitar and vocals and Allen Callaci on vocals (via telephone). Thank you John, for making this magical, musical and healing moment happen. Recorded live at the Great American Music Hall, San Francisco CA, June 29, 2012

Request a free download code by sending an email to

**starfish_songs@pelekinesis.com**

3-song EP available at

https://allencallaci.bandcamp.com/album/heart-like-a-starfish

Donations can be made to:
**Cedars-Sinai for Advanced Heart Disease**
c/o Jon Kobashigawa, MD
8700 Beverly Blvd., Suite 2416
Los Angeles, CA 90048

or by visiting:
**http://giving.cedars-sinai.edu/ways-to-give**

A portion of the proceeds from the sale of this book will be donated to the Cedars-Sinai Heart Institute, where the procedure was performed.

Thank you.

www.ingramcontent.com/pod-product-compliance
Lightning Source LLC
Chambersburg PA
CBHW032127160426
43197CB00008B/540